The U.S. Indo-Pacific Strategy & the Prospect of Forging a New Multipolar World

JIN RAN

Great Wall Publishing

First edition. February 15, 2023.
Copyright © Jin Ran
All Rights Reserved.
This editon published by Mengchen Cultural Communication Group Co., Ltd.
Publishing Coordination: Moontrans

ISBN:978-3-7575-1307-8 (hardback)
ISBN:978-3-7579-0338-1 (ebook)

For permission requests, write to : moontrans@mengchenchina.com

Made with ❤ on the Moontrans Press Platform

www.moontrans.com

To those who strive to make a just and better world...

Abstract

Against the current historical context that the United States is in the process of forging and implementing a grand Indo-Pacific strategy, and that the U.S. has shown its intention to align its strategies toward other regions of the world with its strategic interest in Asia together, this study aims to explore and analyse the critical factors, issues, and mechanisms which would most likely be able to affect the relations among major powers and entities in Europe as well as in the Indo-Pacific region, and to see how possibly the main actors in these two regions could jointly shape a different model of global order, based on their management of and involvements in the core issues identified in this project. The next ten to twenty years will likely be a critical period to see whether a different global system from the current one can be forged, and what it might look like.

Abbreviations

ASEAN	Association of Southeast Asian Nations
ADMM+	ASEAN Defence Ministers' Meeting Plus
AIIB	Asian Infrastructure Investment Bank
ARF	ASEAN Regional Forum
APEC	Asia-Pacific Economic Cooperation
AUKUS	Australia-United Kingdom-United States Trilateral Partnership
BRI	Belt and Road Initiative
CPTPP	Comprehensive and Progressive Agreement for Trans-Pacific Partnership
EAS	East Asia Summit
EEU	Eurasian Economic Union
ECU	Eurasian Customs Union
EU	European Union
FDI	Foreign Direct Investment
G20	Group of Twenty
IMF	International Monetary Fund
IPEF	Indo-Pacific Economic Framework for Prosperity
IEA	International Energy Agency
OPEC	Organization of the Petroleum Exporting Countries
PCA	Partnership and Cooperation Agreement
QUAD	Quadrilateral Security Dialogue
RCEP	Regional Comprehensive Economic Partnership
TPP	Trans-Pacific Partnership
TAC	Treaty of Amity and Cooperation
UN	United Nations
UNHCR	United Nations High Commissioner for Refugees
USAID	U.S. Agency for International Development
USTR	Office of the United States Trade Representative
WB	World Bank
WTO	World Trade Organization

Contents

Introduction

After the world entering the 21st century, a series of incidents happened during the first decade of the new century in the western world such as the terrorist attacks and the global financial crises, as well as the expanded repercussions in the aftermath of these incidents, against the backdrop of the relatively stable economic and security situation in Asia over the same period, precipitated the U.S. strategic shift from other parts of the world to Asia, which led to the framing and implementation of the U.S. "Pivot to Asia" strategy, and further of the Indo-Pacific strategy.

The "Pivot to Asia" strategy was designed by the U.S. government to effectively manage the domestic and international challenges faced by the United States. More precisely, it was set to better serve the U.S. interests in strategic, economic, and security terms through working closely with the U.S. allies and partners particularly based in Southeast Asia and East Asia, and further to help enhance the country's great power status at both regional and global levels.

After the Trump Administration assumed office, the U.S. government adopted an Indo-Pacific strategy, which apparently had expanded further of the strategic and geographic space of the U.S. grand strategy, in comparison to the previous government policy agenda.

With the Biden Administration taking office, apart from having inherited part of the legacies of the Trump government regarding the framework of the Indo-Pacific strategy, the current U.S. government has sought to further enlarge the influence of the Indo-Pacific strategy, as reflected by the fact that it has intended to connect the U.S. strategies toward other regions of the world such as Europe with its strategic interest in the Indo-Pacific region.

So far, to accommodate the implementation of the U.S. Indo-Pacific strategy, in the security area, the U.S. together with Britain and Australia in September 2021 formed a new security grouping, namely the Australia-United Kingdom-United States Trilateral Partnership (AUKUS). Then in February 2022, the U.S. government released a report on its Indo-Pacific strategy. Further, in the economic field, in May 2022, the U.S. led various partners based in the Indo-Pacific region to have launched a new multilateral economic framework, the Indo-Pacific Economic Framework for Prosperity (IPEF). The newly established economic and security frameworks would join other range of bilateral and multilateral frameworks to guide the implementation of the Indo-Pacific strategy in the years ahead.

Over the past more than a decade since the U.S. shifted a large part of its strategic priorities from other regions to Asia, the relevant policies, approaches, and measures adopted by the U.S. governments, under the guidance of a series of strategic arrangements ranging from the U.S. "Re-balance of Asia" strategy to the current Indo-Pacific strategy, have mainly sought to deal with the possible challenges from China, in order to consolidate the U.S. position in the region and beyond.

Along with the process of the U.S. carrying out its Indo-Pacific strategy, differences between China and the U.S., as well as between the two countries and other major powers might emerge from occasion to occasion. Exploring proper means to manage the differences among all the major players, and to prevent them from falling into conflicts is assumed to be an important concern for strategists, politicians, and experts etc.

By bearing the above context in mind, the purpose of this project is to explore the critical factors, relations, and mechanisms which would most possibly be able to affect the likely development of the relations among major powers and entities in both Europe and the Indo-Pacific, and to foresee the trends of how these complex elements and entities would interact with each other, and further cause an impact on the possible forging of a new global order.

To serve this research purpose, this project will attempt to address the following four topics:

● The North Korean Nuclear Issue and the Prospect of A Northeast Asia Regional Security Order

- The U.S., China, and Japan on the Indo-Pacific Strategy
- The Ukraine Crisis & the Prospect of Forging A New European Order and beyond
- The ASEAN Way and the Possible Shaping of An Indo-Pacific Order

This research is designed as a strategic policy studies project, with a particular focus on observing the engagements of major powers and entities, as well as the impacts of their interactions on the prospect of forging a new multi-polar world. The conduction of this research is primarily based on a qualitative exploration, assessment, and analysis of a wide variety of sources, which mainly cover the following:

First, academic materials, consisting of books, journals, reports, and papers published by academic research institutes and think tanks;

Second, data, reports, and fact sheets released by inter-governmental organizations such as the European Union (EU), Association of Southeast Asian Nations (ASEAN), the agencies of the United Nations (UN), and the World Bank (WB) etc., as well as by various government departments such as the White House, and foreign/commerce/defence ministries of relevant governments etc.;

Third, public interviews made by state leaders or other levels of government officials, or by academic experts;

Fourth, speeches or comments made by state leaders or other high-level officials;

Fifth, news released by international media agencies;

Sixth, others.

This research project consists of four chapters. The first chapter aims to explore the impact of the North Korean nuclear issue on the possible shaping of a Northeast Asian regional security order. To meet this purpose, it will more precisely intend to address the these series of questions: what are the crucial factors that have affected the peace process of the Korean Peninsular nuclear issue? how likely the nuclear issue would continue to evolve? whether there could be any new measures to help move the discussions of the parties forward toward the settlement of this issue? and to what extent the evolving trend of the North Korean nuclear issue could have any impacts on the Northeast Asia regional security order and beyond?

Chapter two focuses on investigating the relevance of the U.S., China, and Japan to the Indo-Pacific agenda. More precisely, against the current background that both the U.S. and Japan are in the process of framing and implementing their Indo-Pacific agendas, this chapter aims to observe whether there could be another possibility regarding the likely development of the U.S.-Japan bilateral ties beyond the traditional narratives about the relationship between the two countries, in particular, with respect to the economic and security aspects of their relations. Apart from that, this chapter also tends to examine how possibly the trilateral interactions of the U.S., China, and Japan could affect the outcomes of the Indo-Pacific agenda.

Against the backdrop that the U.S. has shown its intention to align its strategies toward other regions of the world especially Europe with the U.S. strategic interests in Asia together in order to serve a broad and long-term interest of the United States, the management of European affairs by the U.S. including the possible settlement of the Ukraine crisis could carry a significant meaning for major powers and entities in both Europe and Asia. Therefore, chapter three concentrates on assessing the implications of the Ukraine crisis to the four main parties including Ukraine, Russia, the EU, and the U.S. from the social, economic, and strategic dimensions, then based on the understanding of which, to foresee how likely the settlement of the Ukraine crisis could affect the possible forging of a new European order.

Given that the Association of Southeast Asian Nations (ASEAN), by applying a unique ASEAN approach, known as the ASEAN Way, over the past decades has achieved dramatically in maintaining regional peace and contributing to regional economic progress, it is assumed that, under the new historical context that major powers such as India, Japan, China, and the U.S. etc. all have an intention to relate their interests to the Indo-Pacific region, ASEAN, by upholding the ASEAN Way, would likely play a bigger role in helping mediate major power relations, as well as in further contributing to regional peace and progress. Therefore, chapter four tends to examine how likely the ASEAN approach could have an impact on the possible shaping of an Indo-Pacific order and beyond.

CHAPTER 1

How Would the North Korean Nuclear Issue Relate to A Northeast Asia Regional Security Order?

The Korean Peninsula nuclear issue will continue to have an impact on Northeast Asia regional security order. More than three decades ago since North Korea started to develop its nuclear programme, security on the Korean Peninsula has drawn a lot of regional and international attention. The negotiation of the Peninsular nuclear issue over the past years has undergone numerous rounds of ups and downs. The general situation appears that this issue has become more complicated to manage with North Korea's nuclear capacity getting more advanced.

The most recent big breakthrough regarding the negotiation of the nuclear issue on the Korean Peninsula occurred upon former U.S. President Trump's tenure, during which, the leaders of the U.S. and North Korea had held two summits, which happened in Singapore and Vietnam respectively. The warm discussion between the two leaders was cooled down a bit due to their disagreement on denuclearization procedure and verification of denuclearization, yet both leaders kept a good faith in further talks when they left the Vietnam summit in late February 2019. A few months later in June 2019, Trump and Kim had a brief meeting in the demilitarized zone which separates the two Koreas, and agreed to restart the negotiations. The brief meeting also made Trump the first U.S. sitting president to set foot on the North Korean soil.

Since the U.S. President Biden assumed office in January 2021, due to the complexity of the U.S. domestic political situation as well as the changing international environment including the repercussions generated by the COVID-19 pandemic to the world over the past three years, the Biden Administration generally has slowed down the pace of negotiations concerning the Korean Peninsula nuclear issue, and roughly for about one year and half after taking office had taken small steps to approach North Korea. South Korea in the meantime under then President Moon Jae-in had continued to play a mediating role in managing to move the discussions forward.

The South Korean side ever revealed that South Korea and the U.S. had briefly agreed on a framework for ending the Korean War status. To South Korea's claim, the Biden government expressed that the U.S. side was not opposing the idea of signing an End of War declaration, yet the U.S. and South Korea disagreed on the order, timing, and conditions for ending the war. The Biden Administration also expressed its interest in engaging with North Korea toward denuclearization of the Korean Peninsula by following a "step-by-step" approach.[1]

Meanwhile, to respond to South Korea's proposition, the general consensual idea of North Korean officials by then was that before talking about ending the Korean War, it was very significant for the relevant parties to end the hostile policies and measures and double standards, and to make efforts to facilitate good conditions for ending the war.[2]

Following the South Korean leadership transition in May 2022, South Korea has so far been trying a different approach, in contrast to the one adopted by the former South Korean government, in dealing with the North Korean nuclear issue. In the meantime, the Biden Administration has called for recovering negotiations with North Korea, yet the U.S. policies and position toward the Korean Peninsula nuclear issue haven't made any substantial adjustment. In August 2022, the U.S. and South Korea resumed their joint military exercises. Since then, the situation on the Korean Peninsular has been getting intense. The most recently concluded joint air force drills conducted by the U.S. and South Korea before the U.S. midterm election, and in the meantime North Korea's response to that have quickly driven the tension on the Korean Peninsula to a new high.

Generally, the above background roughly reflected the current situation on the Korean Peninsula. Against this backdrop, this research aims to explore further of the relevance of the North Korean nuclear issue to Northeast Asia regional security order and beyond. To meet this general purpose, it tends to more precisely address the following questions: how the Peninsula nuclear issue has evolved and will continue to develop in the years ahead? What major factors have affected the Peninsula peace process? Whether there could be any new measures to move the discussions forward toward the settlement of the North Korean nuclear issue? How likely the development of the Peninsula nuclear issue will affect Northeast Asia regional order and beyond in the future?

In order to better understand how the North Korean nuclear issue has developed to the current stage, this piece will firstly give an overview of the development of this issue in different historical periods. In the meantime, it will tend to develop assessment and analysis on the evolving nature of the issue, alongside the U.S. leadership transitions over the past more than three decades. It would maintain that leadership transitions as well as the policies and approaches taken by the leaders of the main concerned parties having a close relevance to the region have caused a significant impact on the Korean Peninsula peace process. Besides that, the changing global security environment, along with the leadership transitions over the past years, has also been a key factor in affecting the progress of the Korean Peninsula nuclear negotiations. Then, this research will share some alternative measures on how to move up the Peninsula peace process to the next level. Finally, it will foresee in what possible ways the issue can be settled, and in the meantime could have an impact on Northeast Asia regional security order.

1. Management of the North Korean Nuclear Issue in Different Historical Era by the U.S. Government

1.1 Origin of North Korea's Nuclear Programme & the U.S. Handling of It under the Clinton Administration

The primary concern for North Korea to develop nuclear weapons is rooted in the fear of being attacked by the United States. The mentality of fear can be traced back to the Korean War. The U.S. then President Harry Truman ever took into account using atomic bomb in the war. According to Duyeon Kim, since the Korean War, "they (North Koreans) felt that they needed to develop a capability that would deter an American attack", and "the only way for them to survive and not get attacked would be to develop the most powerful weapon on earth, which would be the nuclear bomb."[3]

The development of North Korea's nuclear facilities came into real in the early 1980s. As assisted by the former Soviet Union, North Korea started to build nuclear power plant by then. In the very early stage, North Korea claimed that building nuclear power plant was for a peaceful purpose. By bearing this objective in mind, then in 1985 North Korea joined the Nuclear Nonproliferation Treaty (NPT), the signatories of which were committed to promoting peaceful cooperation on nuclear energy as well as to curbing the dissemination of nuclear weapons and technology.[4]

After the Cold War, as guided by the Strategic Arms Reduction Treaty signed between the U.S. then President George H. W. Bush and the former Soviet leader Mikhail Gorbachev, the U.S. removed nukes from South Korea in September 1991.[5] A few months later in January 1992, North Korea and South Korea also reached a deal, in line with which, they agreed to "not test, manufacture, produce, receive, possess, store, deploy or use nuclear weapons."[6]

The end of the Cold War created a favourable condition for the U.S. to get North Korea to denuclearize. The 1990s under the U.S. former President Clinton's tenure can be a most critical period for settling down the nuclear issue on the Korean Peninsula.

By the end of the Cold War, the U.S. had gained a great proportion of audiences across the globe. In the early 1990s, the U.S. global influence along with its growing soft and hard power had reached a new high. In contrast to the U.S. influence and status, the end of the Cold War apparently put North Korea in an even weaker position. Also,

North Korea's nuclear facilities by then were in the early stage of development, and its nuclear capacity was limited. Therefore, the U.S. obviously had a bigger advantage in setting the agenda for negotiations and in driving the outcomes of negotiations.

Against the above backdrop, right after taking office, the Clinton Administration had managed to move the negotiations with North Korea upward by applying a reconcilable approach. Even though there were discrepancies taking place occasionally, the general situation appeared to be under the U.S. government control; and both parties, North Korea and the U.S., also seemed to be more cooperative in jointly working on the nuclear issue.

In June 1994, the former U.S. President Jimmy Carter paid a visit to North Korea, which made him the first former U.S. leadership to visit North Korea. This visit also created a condition for the U.S. and North Korea to agree on something more concrete based on their previous negotiations. Four months later in October 1994, the two countries signed a deal, namely the Agreed Framework, in compliance with which, North Korea agreed to freeze its nuclear programme; in turn, the U.S. committed to lift sanctions, provide North Korea with aid and oil, as well as help North Korea build two light-water reactors for civilian use.[7]

To fulfill the commitments underlined in the 1994 Agreed Framework, in March 1995, the United States together with Japan and South Korea formed the Korean Peninsula Energy Development Organization (KEDO), which was to "oversee the financing and construction of the two light-water reactors."[8]

For North Korea, in line with the Agreed Framework, the country in September 1999 imposed a missile moratorium. In response, the U.S. lifted economic sanctions on North Korea. It was the first time for the U.S. to do so ever since the Korean War.[9]

Alongside the improvement of the U.S. - North Korea bilateral talks on the nuclear issue, and also due to the series of reconcilable policies and measures taken by South Korea including South Korean President Toh Tae-Woo's "Nordpolitik Policy" as well as President Kim Dae-Jung's "Sunshine Policy", the relationship between the North and the South in the 1990s had opened a new chapter.[10] These policy measures were conducive to the reconciliation process between the two Koreas, and they finally resulted in the first inter-Korean summit ever since the division of the Korean Peninsula between the South Korean President Kim Dae-Jung and North Korean leader Kim Jong-il in June 2000. The summit drew the two Koreas closer and led to a series of exchange activities and cooperation projects, including family reunion and joint commercial and cultural projects etc.[11]

Further to the above, in October 2000, the trips paid by high level officials of North Korea and the United States to each other - North Korean General Jo Myong-rok's visit to the U.S. and then U.S. Secretary of State Madeleine Albright's trip to North Korea - warmed up the discussions even further. The diplomatic exchanges between the two sides resulted in another talk in November the same year.[12]

By the 1990s, the Pyongyang had normalized relationship with a number of countries. It is assumed that the North anticipated to move up the talks with the U.S. on the nuclear issue, and further to normalize relations with the United States. Nevertheless, Clinton's tenure was due shortly after the last talk between the two countries.

Anyway, besides the positive outcomes secured concerning the North Korean nuclear issue under the Clinton Administration, there were also certain flaws in the process of managing this issue. According to Joel Wit, a senior fellow of the Centre for Strategic and International Studies, "the agreement (The Agreed Framework) suffers from a reactor project that is behind schedule, a delay in the planned certification by the International Atomic Energy Agency (IAEA) that is nuclear-free (since certification is linked to the reactor project), and significant funding shortfalls in the agreement's other key component, heavy fuel oil deliveries to the North."[13]

To put a short summary, the Clinton Administration had generally set a good precondition for further engaging with North Korea before shifting power to the next U.S. government. This outcome was mainly attributed to three core factors: a favourable regional and international situation for the U.S. with the end of the Cold War, the positive and active attitude of the leadership of the U.S., South Korea, and North Korea in the 1990s toward the management of the Korean Peninsula nuclear issue, and the generally cooperative stance held by the U.S. and North Korea. These factors decided that the 1990s should be the most critical period for the U.S. and North Korea to build confidence and trust toward settling the nuclear issue on the Korean Peninsula.

1.2 Complication of the North Korean Nuclear Issue under the Bush Term

After the U.S. President Bush took office, the U.S. policy toward North Korea shifted away from a reconcilable approach. The altered U.S. policy in dealing with the North Korean nuclear issue was assumed to have a connection with the U.S. judgment on the security situation both within the U.S. and across the globe after the 9.11 terrorist attacks. Besides that, certain U.S. key political figures' scepticism about North Korea's intention behind the surface also contributed to the U.S. policy shift toward North Korea.

As a result of the 9.11 terrorist attacks, "War on Terror" became a strategic focus of the Bush Administration.The U.S. claimed that North Korea had linkages with Islamic terrorist groups as well as secretly transferred missile technologies to Iran.Hence, a series of actions had been taken by the Bush Administration in the following year after the 9.11 terrorist attacks toward North Korea such as imposing new sanctions, refusing to certify North Korea's compliance to the 1994 Agreed Framework, and suspending oil shipments (which was agreed under the Clinton Administration) to North Korea, and listing North Korea together with Iraq and Iran as an "axis of evil" etc.[14]

In response to the U.S. new measures, North Korea had made a range of moves as well between October 2002 and January 2003 – admitting its running of a uranium enrichment programme to power nuclear weapons, vowing to revive its nuclear plant in Yongbyon, expelling the IAEA inspectors out of the country, and finally withdrawing from the Nuclear Non-proliferation Treaty.[15]

With the breaking down of the 1994 Agreed Framework and North Korea's withdrawal from the NPT, the tension between the U.S. and North Korea for the first time since the end of the Cold War had peaked by around the end of 2002 and the beginning of 2003. It also insinuated that the U.S. had lost control of the situation on the Korean Peninsula.

In order to bring North Korea back to the negotiation table, the diplomatic mechanism of Six Party Talks, which collected South Korea, North Korea, China, Russia, Japan, and the United States together to deal with the North Korean nuclear issue, was initiated in August 2003. Since the Six Party Talks opened, the Bush government had started to soften the U.S. stance a bit toward North Korea.

In the meantime, it is in need to note that the fragile security situation in the Middle East alongside the U.S. invasion of Iraq in 2003 was assumed to have an impact on North Korea's judgment to the country's domestic security situation as well. Security apparently became a primary concern for North Korea by then. Under that circumstance, although South Korea, as guided by President Roh Moo Hyun's "Policy for Peace and Prosperity", had taken a series of measures to lower the temperature on the Korean Peninsula. Nevertheless, South Korea's approach was compromised by the escalation of the security situation on the Korean Peninsula and in other parts of the world.[16] Against this backdrop, the negotiations under the Six Party Talks hadn't gone smoothly at the initial stage.

On 12 September 2005, in order to seek a breakthrough in negotiations with North Korea, the U.S. Treasury Department froze $25 million North Korean fund held in the Macau-based Banco Delta Asia. About a week later on 19 September 2005, the six parties reached a Joint Declaration, in which, North Korea agreed to give up its nuclear programme, comply with the IAEA inspections, and rejoin the NTP. Meanwhile, the U.S. in the Declaration claimed not to attack North Korea.[17]

Then, from October 2006 to the end of President Bush's term, the talks on the nuclear issue had undergone further fluctuations. On 9 October 2006, North Korea shocked other parties by launching its first ever nuclear test, which was carried out underground. North Korea claimed that the nuclear test was a reaction to the U.S. threats, sanctions, and pressure. The UN Security Council condemned North Korea's nuclear test as well as imposed sanctions on the country.[18]

Following that, in February 2007, for implementing the 2005 Declaration, the six parties agreed on an Action Plan, under which, North Korea committed to stop the running of its nuclear facilities in Yongbyon, in exchange, for receiving fifty thousand tons of oil.[19]

Further in June 2007, the U.S. freed the $25 million North Korean fund, which was frozen by the U.S. in September 2005. The six parties then in October released a Joint Statement, according to which, North Korea would uncover all of its nuclear programmes and disable its nuclear facilities, in turn, North Korea would be provided with nine hundred thousand tons of oil. In addition to that, the U.S. agreed to take the North out of the list of state sponsors of terrorism.[20]

In 2008, the U.S. and North Korea made further progress in

implementing the 2007 Joint Statement. North Korea released the information related to its fifteen nuclear sites and nuclear materials. Meanwhile, the Bush Administration issued a plan to remove North Korea from its list of state sponsors of terrorism, as well as waived certain sanctions. By October 2008, the State Department released a preliminary agreement with North Korea on nuclear verification. Nevertheless, before President Bush left office, no agreement was reached due to the disagreement between the two sides on the procedure of verification.[21]

Overall, during Bush's term, along with the changing global security environment, the U.S. policy toward North Korea had undergone a big change from a hardline approach at the very early stage of Bush's tenure to a more reconcilable one following the initiation of the Six Party Talks mechanism. Former President Bush's term can be categorized as a debatable period for the U.S. handling of the Korean Peninsula nuclear issue. Since then, the issue has appeared to become more complicated to deal with, alongside the growing distrust between the U.S. and North Korea. Also because of the distrust, it seemed that North Korea has started to use its nuclear programme as a leverage to meet the country's economic and security needs. Under these circumstances, before absolutely ensuring the country's safety in both economic and security terms, it would be very hard to get North Korea to abandon its nuclear programme.

1.3 Intensification of the Peninsula Nuclear Crisis with the Advancement of North Korea's Nuclear Capacity through Obama's Tenure

After U.S. President Obama came to office, the U.S. had continued to prioritize its strategy on winning the war on terror. Apart from the threats posed by terrorism, the world by then had undergone another big threat, which was the global financial crises started in 2008. The U.S. domestic financial market had been hit deeply by the financial crises. Under those circumstances, to sustain the U.S. global leadership as well as to address the economic and security challenges faced by the country, after assuming office, the Obama Administration had begun by taking a soft and constructive approach generally toward other nations - as Obama pledged in his inaugural address in January 2009, "to all the other peoples and governments who are watching today…know that America is a friend of each nation, and every man, woman and child who seeks a future of peace and dignity."[22]

On the Korean Peninsula nuclear issue, the Obama Administration at the initial stage had tended to deal with it in line with a policy of "strategic patience". The U.S. signaled willingness to resume the Six Party Talks, yet it didn't receive the kind of response from North Korea as the U.S. government expected. In April 2009 around three months after Obama taking office, North Korea launched an Unha-2 rocket. The UN Security Council tightened the sanctions in response to the rocket launch. Then, North Korea claimed not to abide by the agreements secured by the Six Party Talks any more, and vowed to reactivate its already closed nuclear facilities. In the following month, it conducted a second underground nuclear test since its first underground nuclear test taken place in 2006.[23]

Amid the growing tension on the Korean Peninsula, in December 2009, the Obama government officials held a bilateral talk with North Korean officials. However, the escalation of the inter-Korean relations complicated the efforts made by the Obama government in getting North Korea to comply with a range of agreements previously reached by the parties.

By then, a series of factors had contributed to the deteriorating relationship between North Korea and South Korea. The South Korean leadership elected at the end of 2007, compared to his predecessor, much preferred to use a tough line to manage North Korea. Besides that, the Lee Administration failed to meet the agreement made between the two Koreas such as South Korea's commitment related to the "creation of a West Sea Economic Centre in the North Korean port city of Haeju".[24] Meanwhile, the South Korean government also curtailed aid to North Korea.[25]

In addition, the rising tension in the inter-Korean relations also linked with a range of incidents subsequently occurred between the two Koreas including "the shooting of a South Korean tourist in a restricted zone of Mt. Geumgang in July 2008", the nullification of the inter-Korean agreements announced by North Korea in early 2009, as well as the sinking of a South Korean patrol ship, the Cheonan, in March 2010.[26] The sinking of the patrol ship resulted in the death of forty-six South Koreans, which led to strong reciprocal reactions between the two Koreas.

South Korea claimed that the attack of the ship by a North Korean submarine led to its sinking, while North Korea denied any involvement in the accident. The South Korean government demanded apology from North Korea, and imposed new sanctions against the North including banning "North Korean ships from using shipping lanes that crossed ROK territory", and halting "all inter-Korean trade and exchanges outside the inter-Korean Kaesong Industrial Complex (KIC)"[27]

In November 2010, South Korea acted further by carrying out a military drill near the Northern Limit Line, while North Korea in response fired artillery shells at Yeonpyeong Island, which resulted in further casualties of the South Korean side.[28] In the same month, North Korea disclosed its new uranium enrichment programme.[29] From then on for the rest of the time under Lee's presidency, the relationship between the two Koreas had remained tense.[30]

In December 2011, a young leader of North Korea assumed power. Due to the renewed sanctions imposed on North Korea by the UN and the U.S. respectively, North Korea halted the running of its nuclear programme. On 29 February 2012, following a bilateral talk between the U.S. and North Korea in Beijing, North Korea agreed to suspend its Yongbyon uranium enrichment programme, allow the IAEA inspectors back to the country, and impose a moratorium for nuclear and long-range missile tests, in exchange, for receiving tons of food aid. Nevertheless, the agreement later was broken down because of North Korea's new rocket launch.[31]

During Obama's second term, the U.S. Administration had focused on the implementation of its "Pivot to Asia" strategy, which apparently carried a more significant purpose for the United States. Against the backdrop of the U.S. strategic shift to Asia in the aftermath of the global financial crises, with regard to the handling of the Korean Peninsula nuclear issue, apart from continuing to tighten sanctions on North Korea, the U.S. had attempted to seek other means to deal with this matter in the meantime.

Through the same period along with the implementation of the U.S. strategy toward Asia, the inter-Korean relations had undergone further fluctuations and generally been in a very unstable condition through South Korean President Park's term, due to a range of frictions happened between the two Koreas. At the later stage of Park's presidency, South Korean government had tightened its policies toward North Korea.[32] It is assumed that the U.S. "Pivot to Asia" strategy should have had an impact on South Korea as well and somehow precipitated the adjustment of South Korea's policy toward North Korea.

In 2016, following a series of actions taken by South Korea including passing "the North Korea Human Rights Act", signing "a military intelligence sharing agreement with Japan", and declaring "plans to deploy a THAAD missile defense battery to South Korea",[33] the inter-Korean relations was down to a very low level.

The U.S. and South Korea proceeded the consultation on installation of the Theatre High Altitude Area Defense (THAAD) missile system very promptly. In 8 July 2016, the U.S. and South Korea officially signed a deal on installation of it. Due to environment and security concerns, this joint move made by the U.S. and South Korea aroused mass protests in South Korea. It was also strongly opposed by China, because the functioning of the THAAD system, apart from meeting the U.S. strategic interest on the Korean Peninsula and beyond, also posed a challenge to China's security concern. By the end of Obama's second term, the security situation on the Korean Peninsula appeared to be more sensitive.

Overall, under Obama's presidency, the U.S. government had at an initial stage adopted a policy of "strategic patience" in dealing with the nuclear crisis on the Korean Peninsula. Nevertheless, the efforts made by the Obama Administration was undermined by the increasing tension of the inter-Korean relations. Then at a later stage, in particular, during Obama's second term, the Obama government, in accommodating with the U.S. shifting a large part of its strategic priorities from other regions to Asia, had adjusted its policy measures in handling the Peninsular nuclear crisis by applying a different approach in contrast to the approaches adopted by the previous U.S. Administrations.

The U.S. adjustment of policies along with the deteriorating security situation on the Korean Peninsula culminated in the installation of the THAAD missile defence system in South Korea. Nevertheless, this move, instead of being able to bring North Korea to cooperate on denuclearisation, had made the security situation on the Korean Peninsula more vulnerable, as reflected by the reality that, through Obama's tenure, the number of missiles tested under the young leadership of North Korea had surpassed the number of missiles launched by his father and grandfather combined.[34]

1.4 A Breakthrough under Trump's Term

When President Trump came to office in 2017, the U.S. - North Korea relationship was in a very challenging situation apparently. The general atmosphere on the Korean Peninsula was very tense. From the beginning of 2008, the relationship between the two Koreas had generally been in a volatile condition; and meanwhile the unstable inter-Korean relationship somehow had significantly affected the U.S. management of the North Korean nuclear issue through Obama's tenure. By the time when Obama left office, both the U.S.-North Korea relations and the inter-Korean relations had reached a new low point. Against this background, when Trump took office, the Trump government, in contrast to the Bush Administration as well as the Obama government, appeared to face a more challenging task in dealing with North Korea.

Unsurprisingly, during the first year of Trump's presidency, U.S.-North Korea relations had remained tense. The leaders of both countries had for a number of times threatened to each other through exchanging insulting words. Following the sixth nuclear test made by North Korea in September 2017, the Trump Administration in response re-listed North Korea as state sponsors of terrorism.[35]

Amid the on-going challenging security situation on the Korean Peninsula, the South Korean leadership transition as well as the Winter Olympic Games hosted by South Korea in Pyeongchang opened a window for the improvement of the inter-Korean relations. The South Korean government resumed its reconcilable and constructive approach in terms of engaging North Korea. The South invited the North to participate in the Winter Olympic Games, and proposed that the athletes of both countries marched together under one flag in the opening ceremony of the Olympic Games. The good gesture of South Korea was well received by North Korea. With the warming up of the Inter-Korean relations, South Korea had started to play a mediating role between the U.S. and North Korea. Shortly, North Korea, through the South Korean side, sent a message to the U.S., expressing that the North Korean leadership would be willing to meet with the U.S. President to talk about the Peninsula nuclear issue. In March 2018, Trump accepted the invitation and agreed to hold a summit with the

North Korean leader in Pyongyang in May.[36]

In April 2018, the leaders of North Korea and South Korea held a summit at the truce village of Panmunjom, which was the first encounter in 11 years between the heads of the two countries. Through the inter-Korean summit, the leaders of the two Koreas agreed to jointly achieve denuclearization of the Korean Peninsula, and also pledged to turn the armistice treaty into a peace treaty.[37]

In the following month, to pave the way for the scheduled upcoming summit between Trump and Kim, the North Korean side made certain good moves including releasing three U.S. prisoners as well as demolishing the nuclear test site at Punggye-ri.[38]

After further exchanges of information between the U.S. and North Korea, the first Kim-Trump summit was finally scheduled to take place in Singapore in June 2018. The meeting resulted in a Joint Statement, in which, the two leaders were committed to denuclearizing the Korean Peninsula, and pursuing lasting peace, and opening a new chapter for U.S.-North Korea relations - as the North Korean leader said in front of the media, "we had a historical meeting and decided to leave the past behind", and also, as the U.S. President told, "I think our whole relationship with North Korea and the Korean Peninsula is going to be a very much different situation than it has in the past."[39] The Joint Statement also uncovered that concrete actions in compliance with the outcomes secured by the Trump-Kim summit would be followed.[40]

On 18-20 September 2018, the third summit between the heads of South Korea and North Korea took place in Pyongyang. It warmed up the inter-Korean relations even further. Through this summit, the two countries reached another Joint Declaration, through which, to outline the steps for easing tensions, deepening exchanges and cooperation between the two Koreas, and denuclearizing the Korean Peninsula eventually. In the Joint Declaration, North Korea also agreed to permanently close its Dongchang-ri nuclear test site. In addition, alongside the diplomatic statement released, a military declaration was also reached, listing the steps for limiting the joint military exercises between the U.S. and South Korea, and turning the demilitarized zone into a peace zone etc.[41]

The improvement of the inter-Korean relations paved the way for a second Trump-Kim summit, which was scheduled on 27-28 February 2019. By the time when the second summit took place, Trump domestically was facing an impeachment scandal over the Trump Administration's possible linkage with the alleged Russian interference in the U.S. 2016 election. Under this circumstance, the former U.S. President was assumed to urgently need North Korea to make clearer and more substantial commitments toward denuclearization, through which, to help secure even stronger domestic support to his approach in managing the North Korean nuclear issue, while North Korea meanwhile much preferred to denuclearize the Peninsula step by step, in line with which, to move forward sanctions relief and the denuclearization process in parallel.

Besides that, according to the media release, there appeared to be a little misunderstanding between the two sides on each other's wording during the talk - Trump said in front of the media after the summit that "they were willing to denuke a large portion of the areas that we wanted, but we couldn't give up all of the sanctions for that", while a North Korean official claimed that North Korea only demanded "partial" sanctions relief for destroying all the nuclear facilities at the country's Yongbyon nuclear site in exchange.[42]

After all, due to their disagreement on the denuclearization procedure, no joint statement was released after the second Trump-Kim summit. Yet both sides agreed to hold further talks concerning this matter.

A few months later on 30 June 2019, Trump and Kim had another meeting in the demilitarized zone. Their meeting was brief, without many details involved, yet both leaders re-affirmed their commitment to keep the negotiations going.

In the following year, with the spread of the COVID-19 pandemic, fighting the pandemic had become a priority for all the countries across the globe. Apart from that, alongside the U.S. general election held in 2020 as well as the leadership transition shortly thereafter, the pace of communication between North Korea and the U.S. had been slowed down.

Generally, the Trump government, under a very challenging situation on the Korean Peninsula, had managed to make a series of breakthroughs in engaging with North Korea. It prevented further escalation of U.S.-North Korea relations. North Korea reaffirmed the country's commitment to denuclearization through the Panmunjom Declaration upon the inter-Korean summit, as well as through the Joint Statement upon the first Trump-Kim summit.

Besides the above rhetorical statements, North Korea had also taken a series of concrete actions such as destroying its Punggye-ri nuclear test site before the Singapore summit as well as working out the steps together with South Korea for deducing tension, deepening exchanges, and achieving denuclearization.

Generally, even though the negotiations between North Korea and the U.S. were not all going smoothly through Trump's tenure - in particular, during the first year of Trump's term, there had been some very challenging moments, both sides had made efforts to make the situation under control by keeping their conversations going.

Apart from recognizing the progress jointly achieved by the relevant parties, there was also a need to see the underlying challenge in moving the negotiations among the concerned parties, in particular the U.S. and North Korea, up to the next level.

By the time when U.S. President Trump left office, the U.S. and the two Koreas so far hadn't reached a consensus on the procedure of denuclearization, which was proved to be one of the key obstacles having affected the progress of nuclear negotiations as well as of the actions taken toward denuclearization. From the past experiences of engagements between the U.S. and North Korea, once the talks reached a certain point, upon which, both parties were required to make more substantial commitments, the negotiations were found harder to move further, and neither of them was willing to make the first move to fulfil the commitment.

The reason behind the two countries' unwillingness to fulfil the commitment partially lied in the fact that there has been a lack of trust and confidence between North Korea and the U.S. to each other. From North Korea's perspective, it may trust the U.S. President's words such as economic compensation and security guarantee, in exchange, for complete denuclearization, yet there could always be a possibility that the upcoming situation might be beyond the U.S. President's control or willingness to deal with the Peninsula nuclear issue. In the meantime, from the U.S. side, a lot within the U.S. don't believe that North Korea would completely give up its nuclear programme. Therefore, to move the Korean Peninsula peace process to the next stage, more confidence- and trust- building measures should be involved in the diplomatic negotiation and implementation process.

1.5 The Biden Administration: Seeking A "Midpoint

between Strategic Patience and Grand Bargain"[43]

The Biden Administration, for a certain period of time after assuming office, had appeared to prefer a slow and stable approach in handling the Peninsula nuclear issue. After completing the policy review related to North Korea in May 2021, the Biden government ever claimed that the U.S. would seek a "phased agreement" with North Korea to achieve denuclearization.[44] Then in December 2021, the U.S. National Security Adviser Jake Sullivan in an event organized by the Council on Foreign Relations further made clear that the Biden Administration would seek a "step-by-step" approach to engage with North Korea toward denuclearization, and in the meantime expressed the U.S. willingness and readiness to revive negotiations with North Korea.45 This U.S. approach can be described as a middle ground between strategic patience, which characterized the approach adopted by the Obama government in dealing with North Korea for a certain period of time, and grand bargain, which was ever applied by the Trump government during the first year of Trump's tenure in particular.

Besides the above, the U.S. National Security Adviser reaffirmed the U.S. commitment to implementing the June 2018 Joint Statement signed between the U.S. and North Korea. Meanwhile, he also indicated that sanctions will remain in place; and the U.S. would coordinate with its key Asian allies to promote sanctions implementation.[46]

Around the same period, South Korea had been very active in engaging with both the U.S. and North Korea for reviving the formal talks between the two Koreas and between the U.S. and North Korea. In addition to that, South Korea had been in close contact with China, the U.S., and North Korea for jointly pursuing a goal of ending the war status on the Korean Peninsula.

Then South Korean President Moon Jae-in had, on a few occasions, including upon his participation in the 76th United Nations General Assembly, upon his visit to Australia, as well as upon the UN Peacekeeping Ministerial Meeting hosted by South Korea, proposed the idea of signing an End of War Declaration, and expressed South Korea's commitment to working closely with the concerned parties to achieve that goal.

From the South Korean perspective, ending the war status on the Korean Peninsula apparently was taken by the Moon government as a very significant starting point toward eventual denuclearization; and signing a political declaration for ending the war could be conducive to the progress of denuclearization.

In response to South Korea's proposal, although the U.S. was not opposed the idea of ending the Korean War, the U.S. National Security Adviser also indicated that the U.S. and South Korea viewed differently on the order, timing, and conditions for signing an End of War Declaration.[47]

In the meantime, there had been some discussions on the concept of End of War Declaration in the scholarly field. Some experts viewed that denuclearization or at least a clear roadmap toward denuclearization should come first before reaching an agreement on ending the war on the Korean Peninsula.[48] Some argued that human rights condition in North Korea should be taken into consideration before signing an End of War Declaration.[49]

On the North Korean side, the officials of the country had for a few times expressed North Korea's position on the matter of ending the Korean War status. The general idea by then was that before talking about ending the war, the timing and conditions for doing that needed to be taken into account. Besides that, there was a need for relevant parties to show mutual respect, give up the double standard, and abandon the hostile policy and words toward North Korea etc.[50]

On the same issue, China is willing to keep close contact with all other parties and to continue to play a constructive role in the discussions of ending the war and achieving peace on the Korean Peninsula. In a meeting in early December 2021 between then Director of the Office of the Central Foreign Affairs Committee Yang Jiechi and a senior South Korean official, Mr. Yang expressed China's support in improving the inter-Korean relations, and proposed to address the Peninsular nuclear issue through dialogue and consultation in line with the "dual track and proceeding in parallel" approach and the "step-by-step" principle, to safeguard peace and stability, and to play a constructive role in helping achieve the long term peace on the Korean Peninsula.[51]

From the relevant parties' responses to South Korea's proposition for ending the war status on the Korean Peninsula, apparently, the parties, in particular, North Korea and the U.S. for the time being had different concerns about the idea of putting the Korean War to an end. Nevertheless, they did appear to have briefly agreed on a common approach toward denuclearization, which was to pursue denuclearization step by step, in line with which, the actions related to sanctions relief, compensation, and denuclearization would be processed in parallel.

To move the Korean Peninsula peace process forward, the important issue is to get the parties to go back to the negotiation table and discuss the terms, conditions, and steps toward denuclearization. However, both North Korea and the U.S. have made certain new moves since the beginning of 2022. North Korea has made new missile launches; and meanwhile, the U.S. has imposed new sanctions. Since late August 2022, the security situation on the Korean Peninsula has been facing a new round of escalation, alongside the resumption of the U.S.-South Korea joint military exercises, and in the meantime North Korea's responses to a series of collective operations made by the U.S. and South Korea by making a number of new missile tests. As a counteraction to the U.S.-South Korea joint air force drills happened from 31 October to 6 November, North Korea on 2 November 2022 fired 23 missiles - the largest number so far in a single day.[52]

On the South Korean side, as a result of the different views held by the major concerned parties on the procedure, timing, and conditions of denuclearization, before former President Moon Jae-in left office, no further substantial progress related to the negotiations on the Peninsula nuclear issue was made. After South Korean President Yoon Suk-yeol took office, the South Korean government so far has preferred to apply a range of different policy measures, in contrast to those adopted by the previous government, in dealing with the inter-Korean relations and the North Korean nuclear issue. Given the recent new round of tension on the Korean Peninsula, how long it would take for the main concerned parties to go back to the negotiation table and to jointly achieve new breakthroughs toward denuclearization partially will depend on whether and how likely the South Korean government would adjust their measures toward North Korea in the next steps. Apart from that, in order to enable the U.S. to exercise a certain degree of domination on the Korean Peninsula, how likely the U.S. strategy - currently the Indo-Pacific strategy - can be implemented would also have a relevance to the promotion of the Peninsula peace process in the coming steps.

Generally, the above part of this research has just made a historical overview of the development of the Korean Peninsula nuclear crisis, mixed with assessments and analysis on the core factors that have greatly affected the Korean Peninsula peace process over the past more than three decades. From what have been observed, we can see that the evolving trend of the security situation on the Korean Peninsula cannot be isolated from the changing security environment in other parts of the world. In addition, leadership transitions over the past decades within the relevant parties, in particular, the United States, South Korea, and North Korea have been proved to have a big impact on the development of the Peninsula nuclear issue.

In the coming years, leadership transitions will continue, and the security situation in various parts of the globe will be undergoing further changes or adjustments. Besides these two key factors, another matter, which is very much related to the sensitivity of the North Korean nuclear crisis itself, shouldn't be ignored as well in promoting the Peninsula peace process in the coming years. Through all these years of management of this matter by the relevant parties, the North Korean nuclear issue has appeared to be getting more sensitive to deal with. The problem of distrust between the two main parties, the U.S. and North Korea, hasn't been properly addressed over the past years. The lack of enough confidence and trust between the two countries has turned the management of the Peninsula nuclear issue into a pattern characterized by constant circulation, along with which, should the negotiations and actions be progressed to a certain point, what have been achieved by the parties would risk being reversed.

2. Possible Measures for Moving forward the Peninsula Peace Process

2.1 Taking the Relevant Parties' Core Interests and Concerns as A Starting Point

In the coming steps, in order to seek new breakthroughs toward denuclearization of the Korean Peninsula, there is a need for the main stakeholders to seek more alternative means to jointly manage the Peninsula peace process including trying to undermine the repercussions possibly generated by the three main factors - policy shifts alongside leadership transitions, the unpredictable security environment in Northeast Asia and other regions of the world, as well as the issue of distrust between the main concerned parties. To achieve that, the starting point is to understand better of the core interests and concerns of the parties having a close relevance to the Peninsula nuclear issue, based on which, to think about how to better balance and meet the interests of them.

The parties, which are mostly concerned about the security situation on the Korean Peninsula, consist of the two Koreas, Japan, Russia, China, and the U.S.. A brief consensus held by them is to denuclearize the Korean Peninsula, yet they, due to the different concerns held by the U.S. and North Korea on the procedure of denuclearization, so far haven't been able to reach a consensus on how to achieve denuclearization.

According to Joel Wit, the U.S. strategy on the Korean Peninsula mainly bears four purposes: maintaining regional stability, preventing nuclear proliferation, encouraging inter-Korean interactions, and ensuring the stableness of the U.S.-ROK alliance relationship.[53] Apparently, maintaining the U.S. influence and strategic relevance on the Korean Peninsula and in Northeast Asia has been a key strategic priority of the United States. Possessing nuclear weapons by North Korea, besides security concerns, can be one of the major threats to the U.S. interest in maintaining its strategic relevance in Northeast Asia. Only by denuclearizing the Korean Peninsula, should the U.S. sense more certainty in managing the security situation in the region. Simply put, denuclearizing North Korea without undermining the U.S. strategic relevance in Northeast Asia should be the primary concern of the United States.

For China, given the geographical proximity between China and the two Koreas, security on the Peninsula is directly related to China's domestic security in various terms as well as to China's security concern in the region. Therefore, peace and stability on the Korean Peninsula is important for China. There is no reason for China not to pay a special attention to the Peninsula nuclear issue.

For North Korea and South Korea, their ultimate goal is to achieve unification, while at the current stage and in the foreseeable future, the two Koreas would take traditional security into particular consideration. In addition to that, economic security would also be a primary concern for North Korea.

For Russia, its main concern in relation to the Korean Peninsula nuclear issue and more broadly to the security situation in Northeast Asia would generally be complementary to China's. Both countries would attach great significance to peace and stability in this region.

As for Japan, apart from traditional security concerns led by the Peninsula nuclear crisis, Japan has been striving to become a more important actor in economic and security affairs in Northeast Asia and beyond. The purpose of making all these efforts is to enable Japan to be a more independent and influential actor in regional and global affairs rather than solely rely on the protection and influence of the United States.

By taking the above main stakeholders' primary concerns into account, in the coming years, it is assumed that, as far as the main concerns of the relevant parties can be properly met and balanced from occasion to occasion, should there be a greater possibility for them to jointly find better solutions to move up the Korean Peninsula peace process. To achieve this goal, the parties need to create a platform, through which, to express their concerns and pursue their interests. Therefore, an alternative solution for addressing the North Korean nuclear crisis in a long run is to let liberal institutionalism rather than offensive realism play a more crucial role in guiding states' policy making and approaches in handling the Peninsula nuclear crisis. More precisely, promoting regional institutional building and forming a special body to focus on dealing with the Korean Peninsula nuclear issue can be an alternative solution to better meet the concerns and interests of relevant parties.

There are experts having already advised to establish a permanent institution in Northeast Asia to oversee the denuclearization process of the Korean Peninsula, as well as other future security issues in the region to a larger extent.[54]

2.2 An Alternative Way Out: Promoting and Optimizing Regional Institutional Building or Improving the Function of Great Power Coordination Mechanism?

Given that the significance of regionalism, regional cooperation and development, and regional peace and stability etc. will further be highlighted in the future in terms of their relevance and contribution to the overall global cooperation, peace, and stability. Therefore, it is assumed that setting up a special body in the security area in Northeast

Asia to deal with security issues in both traditional and non-traditional terms from a long-term perspective would be necessary.

If the timing and conditions for establishing a permanent body are not mature, the concerned parties may take into consideration forming an ad hoc institution with a priority on addressing the Korean Peninsula nuclear issue. Then, the ad hoc one can be turned into a permanent body to focus on handling a wider range of security issues in Northeast Asia, which may cover the aspect of traditional security as well as of economic, energy, and environmental security etc., should the conditions and timing get mature.

The ad hoc body forged for managing the Peninsula nuclear issue is supposed to be different from the Six Party Talks, even though it may need to learn certain lessons and experiences from the Six Party Talks. This special institution should be a fully institutionalized body including possessing the executive power to enforce or implement the decisions agreed by its members. Also, its functions should be designed to cover a much broader range of aspects such as consulting and coordinating with all the stakeholders, mediating the relations among them, drafting the roadmap toward denuclearization, and tracking the procedures of verification and denuclearization etc. Despite the fact that the special security body remains neutral among all its members, it does have the power to decide which party/parties to consult with under a special circumstance or at a particular stage. All in all, the special body is supposed to take the lead in all the matters related to denuclearization.

Over the past more than three decades, the U.S. has been intending to address the Korean Peninsula nuclear issue mainly by applying a realist approach. After all these years of management of this matter, the two major parties, the U.S. and North Korea, alongside the growing distrust between them, appeared to have been dragged into a circle. Therefore, under the current circumstances, setting up a special institution could help create certainty, steadiness, and reliability by undermining the vulnerability and uncertainty possibly caused by leadership transition, unstable external environment, as well as other series of internal and external factors. Overall, the conditions that the special body tends to create are conducive to confidence- and trust-building among all stakeholders.

The six parties having ever engaged in the Peninsula peace process can be the founding members of a special security body in Northeast Asia. At the current stage, they generally agreed to denuclearize the

Korean Peninsula by adhering to a "step-by-step" approach. Moving the negotiations forward and implementing the statements or declarations agreed by the parties need a great deal of technical skills. It is expected that the creation of a special security body could possess enough skills in manoeuvring a complicated situation, and help move up the Korean Peninsula peace process by properly balancing the different concerns held by the stakeholders.

Another alternative solution for settling down the Korean Peninsula nuclear issue would mainly be involved in the function of great power coordination mechanism. More precisely, the great powers would agree on a special arrangement on the Korean Peninsula nuclear issue in the first place, and jointly provide North Korea with security guarantee as well as help North Korea's economy step by step, in exchange, for a nuclear-free North Korea.

Then the final question coming up would be related to how likely the management of the Korean Peninsula nuclear issue in the coming years could affect Northeast Asia regional security order?

3. The Korean Peninsula Nuclear Issue and Northeast Asia Regional Security Order

The North Korean nuclear issue will likely have an impact on the security order in Northeast Asia in a few possible ways. One possibility could be that if a special security institution can finally help settle down the Peninsula nuclear crisis, the practice jointly developed by the six parties will not only be of a further enrichment of the theory of liberal institutionalism, but also help generate valuable precedence for addressing future security issues in Northeast Asia as well as security threats in other regions.

By achieving the goal of denuclearization of the Korean Peninsula, it would prove that balancing the core concerns and interests held by various parties through institutional management is possible, as far as the stakeholders hold a cooperative attitude toward security issues as well as other range of matters.

The Chinese leadership ever indicated that the Pacific is vast enough to include both China and the United States in it. Therefore, in the end, the settlement of the Peninsula nuclear issue shouldn't be a zero-sum game between the U.S. and North Korea, neither should it be a zero-sum game between China and the U.S., as well as between North Korea and South Korea. From a very long run, the unification of the two Koreas will not be a dream under that future circumstance.

A second possibility would be that the major parties would go down a path by allowing offensive realism to continue to dominate the policies and approach related to the Korean Peninsula nuclear issue. In that case, the distrust between the parties would remain and likely keep growing. Then the Korean Peninsula peace process would likely continue to undergo the similar ups and downs, as the parties have experienced over the past more than thirty years.

A third one would be related to the outcomes generated by the function of great power coordination mechanism. Under this scenario, great power coordination mechanism would be allowed to have a main play in helping solve the Korean Peninsula nuclear crisis, and in line with it, great powers would work out a special arrangement concerning the settlement of the North Korean nuclear issue including offering security guarantee to North Korea. Then the possible outcomes led by great power consultation would also be conducive to great powers' efforts in finding a way to peacefully coexist from a long-term perspective, and in developing a new type of great power relations in the 21st century, as well as in jointly contributing to the forging of a Northeast Asia regional security order.

A fourth one might be that the major parties would lose patience to each other, and finally decide to take a more drastic means like launching a war to settle down the nuclear crisis. The situation and consequences generated by a war in that case would be hard to imagine.

Conclusion

To better understand how the North Korean nuclear issue has affected and will continue to have an impact on Northeast Asia regional security order, this analytical study has begun by reviewing how the Korean Peninsula peace process has evolved over the past more than three decades. In the 1990s, the U.S. had taken a lead in interacting with North Korea concerning the Peninsula nuclear issue. Then for a certain period of time between 2003 and 2009 along with the initiation of the Six Party Talks, the six parties including the two Koreas, Japan, Russia, China, and the U.S., with the involvement of the U.N. Security Council, had jointly managed the Korean Peninsula nuclear crisis. Following North Korea's withdrawal from the Six Party Talks in 2009, the function of this mechanism was suspended. Then, once again the U.S. has been back in the main position in seeking various means to engage with North Korea including working with its allies to impose pressure on the country.

Even though the relevant parties have managed to make certain breakthroughs in different stages, there will still be full of uncertainties and challenges in the years ahead, mainly due to the fact that the fundamental issue of distrust remained between the two major parties, the United States and North Korea, hasn't been properly managed over the past years. The root cause behind the distrust is complicated. This study has assessed three major factors having significantly affected the Korean Peninsula peace process, including the fluctuation of policies and approaches toward the management of this issue alongside leadership transitions, and unstable external security environment across the globe, as well as the growing sensitivity of the North Korean nuclear issue itself.

In the coming years, to proceed the Peninsula peace process to a new level, there is a need for the concerned parties to prioritize confidence- and trust- building measures. To cultivate confidence and trust among the main stakeholders, their concerns and interests should be taken into special consideration and be properly balanced in the meantime. This analysis assumed that promoting and optimizing institutional building at the regional level, in line with which, to establish a special body to focus on managing the Korean Peninsula issue could be an alternative solution for addressing the North Korean nuclear crisis. Apart from that, improving the function of great power coordination mechanism could also be a way for handling this issue.

After all, regardless of what path or approach the concerned parties would choose to settle down the Korean Peninsula nuclear issue ultimately, it would significantly influence Northeast Asia regional security order and beyond.

Notes

1. Ji Da-gyum, "U.S. Seeks 'step-by-step' Approach toward Denucle arization', *The Korea Herald,* 19 December 2021, http://www.kore aherald.com/view.php?ud=20211219000150; Also see Nezam Joshua, "An End-of-War Declaration on the Korean Peninsula: Pursuing a Phased Agreement with the Goal of Complete Denuclearization", *Interview with Shin-wha Lee*, The National Bureau of Asian Research, 3 December 2021, https://www.nbr.org/publication/an-end-of-war-declaration-on-the-korean-peninsula-pursuing-a-phased-agreement-with-the-goal-of-com plete-denuclearization/

2. Guan Junran, "Moon Jae-in Would Declare the 'End of War Declaration' upon the Winter Olympic Games?"- Differences on the Terms of Denuclearization still Remain, *Tencent,* 9 December 2021, https://new.qq.com/omn/20211209/20211209A053NA00.html

3. Cited from Boghani Priyanka, "The U.S. and North Korea on the Brink: A Timeline", *PBS,* 28 February 2019, http://www.pbs.org/wgbh/frontline/article/the-u-s-and-north-korea-on-the-brink-a-timeline/

4. Albert Eleanor, "North Korean Nuclear Negotiations", *Council on Foreign Relation,* 2 July 2019, https://www.cfr.org/timeline/north-korean-nuclear-negotiations

5. Ibid.

6. Cited from Albert Eleanor, "North Korean Nuclear Negotiations".

7. Ibid.

8. Ibid.

9. Ibid.

10. Wertz Daniel, "Inter-Korean Relations", *ISSUE BRIEF*, The National Committee of North Korea, 2017.

11. Ibid.

12. Albert Eleanor, "North Korean Nuclear Negotiations".

13. Wit Joel, "The United States and North Korea", *The Brookings,* 15 March 2001, http://www.brookings.edu/research/the-united-states-and-north-korea/

14. Albert Eleanor, "North Korean Nuclear Negotiations".

15. Ibid.

16. Wertz Daniel, "Inter-Korean Relations".

17. Albert Eleanor, "North Korean Nuclear Negotiations".
18. Ibid.
19. Ibid.
20. Ibid.
21. Ibid.
22. The White House, "President Barack Obama's Inaugural Address", 21 January2009, https://obamawhitehouse.archives.gov/blog/2009/01/21/president-barack-obamas-inaugural-address
23. Albert Eleanor, "North Korean Nuclear Negotiations".
24. Wertz Daniel, "Inter-Korean Relations".
25. Ibid.
26. Ibid.
27. Ibid.
28. Ibid.
29. Albert Eleanor, "North Korean Nuclear Negotiations".
30. Wertz Daniel, "Inter-Korean Relations".
31. Albert Eleanor, "North Korean Nuclear Negotiations".
32. Wertz Daniel, "Inter-Korean Relations".
33. Ibid.
34. Albert Eleanor, "North Korean Nuclear Negotiations".
35. Ibid.
36. Boghani Priyanka, "The U.S. and North Korea on the Brink: A Timeline".
37. Albert Eleanor, "North Korean Nuclear Negotiations".
38. Ibid.
39. Cited from Boghani Priyanka, "The U.S. and North Korea on the Brink: A Timeline".
40. Ibid.
41. Albert Eleanor, "North Korean Nuclear Negotiations".
42. Cited from Boghani Priyanka, "The U.S. and North Korea on the Brink: A Timeline".
43. Council on Foreign Relations, "A Conversation with Jake Sullivan", http://www.cfr.org/event/conversation-jake-sullivan; also see Ji Da-gyum, "U.S. Seeks 'step-by-step' Approach toward Denuclearization', *The Korea Herald,* 19 December 2021, http://www.k oreaherald.com/view.php?ud=20211219000150
44. Nezam Joshua, "An End-of-War Declaration on the Korean Peninsula: Pursuing a Phased Agreement with the Goal of Complete Denuclearization", *Interview with Shin-wha Lee*, The National Bureau of

Asian Research, 3 December 2021, https://www.nbr.org/publica tion/an-end-of-war-declaration-on-the-korean-peninsula-pursuing-a-phased-agreement-with-the-goal-of-complete-denuclearization/

45. Council on Foreign Relations, "A Conversation with Jake Sullivan", http://www.cfr.org/event/conversation-jake-sullivan

46. Ibid.

47. Nezam Joshua, "An End-of-War Declaration on the Korean Peninsula: Pursuing a Phased Agreement with the Goal of Complete Denu clearization", *Interview with Shin-wha Lee*, The National Bureau of Asian Research, 3 December 2021,https://www.nbr.or g/publication/an-end-of-war-declaration-on-the-korean-peninsula-pursuing-a-phased-agreement-with-the-goal-of-complete-denuclearization/

48. Ibid.

49. Belfer Center, http://www.belfercenter.org/publication/policy-public-dipl omacy-north-korea

50. Guan Junran, "Moon Jae-in Would Declare the 'End of War Declaration' upon the Winter Olympic Games?"- Differences on the Terms of Denuclearization still Remain, *Tencent,* 9 December 2021, https://new.qq.com/omn/20211209/20211209A053NA00.html

51. Ibid.

52. Seo Yoonjung, Jeong Sophie, Ogura Junko, and Whiteman Hilary, "North Korea Fired the Highest Number of Short-range Missiles in A Day, Says South Korea", *CNN,* 2 November 2022, https://edition.cnn.com /2022/11/01/asia/north-korea-missiles-wednesday-intl-hnk/index.html

53. Wit Joel, "The United States and North Korea", *The Brookings.* 15 March 2001, http://www.brookings.edu/research/the-united-states-and-north-korea/

54. Yoshida Fumihiko and Paik Haksoon in a policy proposal titled "From Peace on the Korean Peninsula to a Northeast Asia Nuclear Weapon Free Zone" proposed some ideas in great details on the formulation of a special institution in Northeast Asia to focus on addressing security issues in this region, *Journal for Peace and Nuclear Disarmament,* VOL.3/NO.1:123-128, 2020,
https://www.tandfonline.com/doi/epdf/10.1080/25751654.2020.1747910?needAccess=true&role=button

CHAPTER 2

The United States, China, and Japan on the Indo-Pacific Strategy

Among a variety of factors, which could significantly affect the affairs in the Indo-Pacific region, the likely development of U.S.-Japan relations should be one of them. Japan's role in the prospect of contributing to the forging of an Indo-Pacific order and beyond cannot be underestimated from a long-term perspective.

Since the end of WWII, Japan's policy orientation, in particular in relation to economic and security affairs, has been greatly influenced by the overall policy agenda of the United States. Generally, Japanese policy makers have been attempting to find a way to align Japan's interests with those of the U.S., and to accommodate the U.S. demands from occasion to occasion. Nevertheless, through the same period, Japan has never stopped its efforts in growing its own capacity by applying a variety of means in order to make the country more like a "Normal State".

During the former U.S. President Trump's term, the U.S. has started to focus on framing an Indo-Pacific strategy; and in the meantime, Japan has also sought to formulate the country's own Indo-Pacific agenda. The conceptual meaning of the Indo-Pacific strategy was initially connected to a speech made by the former Japanese Prime Minister Shinzo Abe upon his official visit to India back in 2007. Abe, in his address to the Indian Congress, firstly proposed an idea of "the confluence of the two seas" - the Pacific and the Indian Oceans - and to make them be the seas of freedom and prosperity for a broader Asia.[1] Japan, in line with this proposition, expected to deepen ties and enhance cooperation with countries sharing the similar fundamental values. Later, this initial idea was developed and characterized by Japan as a "free and open Indo-Pacific vision". Meanwhile, alongside the U.S. strategic adjustment, the concept of Indo-Pacific was also adopted by the Trump Administration, and further developed to an "Indo-Pacific strategy".

Even though both Japan and the U.S. have an interest in carrying out the Indo-Pacific strategy/vision, the two countries have tended to interpret this term differently. The U.S. would take it more as a part of the U.S. overall global strategy, through which, to project the U.S. influence in the Indo-Pacific region, to help strengthen the U.S. alliance relationship, and to sustain the U.S. global leadership and hegemony.

As for Japan, it appears that the Japanese government has attempted to make this term more inclusive by defining it as a vision rather than a strategy as well as by including the developing countries based in Africa and the Middle East into the framework of Japan's Indo-Pacific vision, with an obvious purpose of expecting, through it, to facilitate a more enabling and sustainable environment to meet Japan's economic and security interests from a broad and long-term sense.

Under the above circumstances, from a long-term perspective, against the backdrop that both the U.S. and Japan are interested in carrying out their Indo-Pacific agendas, how likely will the U.S.-Japan bilateral engagements continue to develop? By applying what possible means would both the U.S. and Japan tend to implement their Indo-pacific agendas respectively? How likely could the Indo-Pacific strategy affect the status of both Japan and the U.S., and also Japan's posture toward its neighbours in this region? How likely could China have an impact on the framing and implementation of the Indo-Pacific strategy?

By bearing the above questions in mind, this piece aims to explore whether there could be another possibility regarding the likely development of U.S.-Japan bilateral ties, in particular, concerning the collaboration between the two countries on economic and security issues, as well as to observe how possibly the trilateral engagements of the U.S., China, and Japan could influence the outcomes of the Indo-Pacific agenda, and also the possible shaping of an Indo-Pacific order and beyond.

To meet the above research purpose, this piece will begin by giving a brief historical overview of the U.S.-Japan bilateral interactions on security and economic issues. Then, it will try to analyse in greater details of the mentality of U.S.-Japan bilateral cooperation in these two areas through the past years as well as in the future, based on which, to further explore the possible trend of U.S.-Japan bilateral relations in the years ahead under the context of framing and implementing the Indo-Pacific agenda by both countries. Finally, it will try to understand in what way the China factor could have an impact on the outcomes of the Indo-Pacific agenda.

1. A Brief Historical Overview of U.S.-Japan Bilateral Interactions on Economic, Trade, and Security Issues

In the economic and trade domain, for a long period through the 1970s to the first half of the 1990s, the United States and Japan had been each other's most crucial cooperative partners. Even nowadays, the linkages between the two countries in the economic area are still considered significant, yet the degree of significance in U.S.-Japan economic cooperation has been relatively deduced over the years, with other countries including the emerging economies having turned into important economic partners of the two countries respectively.

The ever growing economic connectivity between the U.S. and Japan had made the U.S. the largest merchandise importer of Japan by the late 1980s, and Japan the second largest U.S. merchandise export market at the same time.[2] Yet, along with the increasing connection between the two economies, frictions had also emerged and been gradually becoming a more serious concern for both countries, ranging from product- and sector- specific disputes to structure/Polic ies/regulations- related problems.

In 1971, the U.S. for the first time had a $6.1 billion merchandise trade deficits with Japan; from then on, the number had kept growing, and reached $810 billion in 2017.[3] Throughout this period, during 1980s, the share of the U.S. deficits with Japan out of the U.S. total deficits had surged most quickly; and then it peaked in 1991, accounting for around 54% of the U.S. total deficits by then.[4]

In response to the frictions raised between the U.S. and Japan from the 1970s to the beginning of the 21st century, the decision makers of the two countries, under the pressure imposed by the U.S. side, had jointly managed to form a series of special bilateral frameworks from time to time. The main objective of these frameworks was set to facilitate fair competition and help increase the presence of the U.S. products and services in the Japanese market through promoting market access.

The outcomes achieved through carrying out these frameworks were debatable. For instance, under the Market-Oriented Sector-Specific Framework introduced by the Reagan Administration, a study conducted by the General Accounting Office in 1988 showed that the U.S. exports in the selected sectors - excluding auto parts - more or less had increased, yet the improved market access to Japan hadn't led to a big surge in the U.S. exports to Japan,[5] given that "macroeconomic trends and other factors also play a role that could trump market access",[6] as argued by William Cooper, a Specialist in International Trade and Finance with the U.S. Congressional Research Service. Similarly, the implementation of other series of special frameworks between the U.S. and Japan in the years thereafter had also exhibited disputable outcomes.

Generally, under the U.S. management of the U.S.-Japan bilateral economic relations through the special frameworks signed between the two countries, certain improvements, more from the U.S. perspective, had been made, yet some fundamental issues between the U.S. and Japan such as regulatory practices, or sector-specific frictions related to trade in autos and auto parts, or trade imbalances etc. have remained and been occasionally raised up by the U.S. side. [7]

With respect to the U.S. handling of the U.S.-Japan frictions on economic and trade issues, some observers maintained that certain restrictive measures imposed by the U.S. on Japan through the 1980s to the 1990s were the main cause of the slowdown of the Japanese economy after then.

In the mid-1990s, Both the U.S. and Japan had further diversified or expanded their economic partners. Along with the changing security situation in Northeast Asia and the Taiwan Strait, economic collaboration and frictions raised in the economic domain between the two countries have since then been relatively sidelined; and security cooperation has gradually become more prominent in the U.S.-Japan bilateral relations.

As for U.S.-Japan security collaboration, after WWII, the Japanese post-war constitution, which was drafted by the U.S., set the limits in Japan's defence capacity. Japan has since then mostly relied on the U.S. for national defence. The U.S.-Japan Treaty of Mutual Cooperation Security laid the groundwork of the alliance relationship in defence between the two countries, according to which, the U.S. was permitted to set military base in Japan, in return, Japan would be protected by the U.S., if under attack.[8]

Afterward, in line with the changing regional and global security environment, as well as with the adjustment of the U.S. overall strategy from time to time, the two countries had for a couple of times furthered their defence cooperation by focusing on augmenting Japan's defence capacity in particular.

After the Korean War, in 1954, Japan established the Japan Self-Defence Forces (JSDF), which was taken as Japan's military but had very limited operational capacity. Then, to serve the U.S. Cold War policy, in 1978, the two countries signed the first bilateral Guidelines for Defence Cooperation, which allowed the two sides to conduct joint training. Further to that, in response to the challenges posed by the North Korean nuclear programme, and also by the crisis in the Taiwan Strait, the U.S. and Japan for the first time in 1997 revised their bilateral Guidelines for Defence Cooperation, under which, Japanese forces were enabled to carry out military operations both on the home hand of Japan and in the surrounding areas.[9]

With the former Japanese Prime Minister Shinzo Abe taking office, in particular, during Abe's second term, Japan had taken significant steps in upgrading its defence capacity, ranging from creating the National Security Council in 2013, releasing its first National Security Strategy later in the same year, relaxing Japan's arms exports policy, increasing defence spending, to further revising the U.S.-Japan Defence Guidelines.[10]

In addition to that, the Abe Administration had made enormous efforts in an attempt to reinterpret the Japanese Constitution, and in the meantime to seek legislative support for reforming Japan's national defence, in particular, with respect to lifting the ban on the right of collective self-defence. Nevertheless, due to public protests and opposition to the series of defence reforms proposed by the Abe Cabinet, in addition to the contentious debates raised within the legislative body regarding this matter in the meantime, finally the legislation did not fully empower Japanese forces the unrestricted right to exercise collective self-defence.[11]

Generally, the above narratives have briefly pictured the U.S.-Japan bilateral engagements in the economic and security areas over the past decades. Then how to understand the motivation and mentality of both countries behind the U.S.-Japan bilateral collaboration in the past as well as in the years ahead?

2. Understanding the Mentality of the U.S. and Japan in the U.S.-Japan Bilateral Relations

Under the context of carrying out the Indo-Pacific agenda by both the U.S. and Japan in the years ahead, from the U.S. perspective, as usual, it would want Japan to share more burdens. Thus, the U.S. would aim to further increase Japan's capacity. Nevertheless, in the meantime, the U.S. would not allow Japan to keep growing beyond the U.S. interests and control.

By recalling what had happened in history regarding the U.S. handling of the U.S.-Japan collaboration in a number of areas, it is easy to find out that once Japan's capacity reached to a certain point, which challenged the U.S. interest or was beyond the U.S. control, Japan had been pressed to make policy adjustment. The same logic will be applied as well in the process of implementing the Indo-Pacific strategy.

From the Japanese side, the country appears to have a more complicated mentality toward the U.S.-Japan bilateral relations. On the one hand, some Japanese politicians would prefer to bound Japan's strategies and policies with those of the U.S. together, mostly due to security concerns. Thus, in order to avoid being abandoned by the U.S., Japan has constantly made commitments to meet the U.S. demands from time to time. For instance, to accommodate the U.S. strategic shift from other regions to Asia, in the security arena, Japan had ever taken important steps in reforming its national defence; and in the economic field, unlike other key allies of the United States, Japan had been more cautious toward China-initiated multilateral mechanisms such as the Asian Infrastructure Investment Bank (AIIB) and the Belt and Road Initiative (BRI), even though former Japanese Prime Minister Abe at a later stage also expressed Japan's open attitude toward joining the AIIB as well as expanding collaboration with the BRI.[12]

On the other hand, Japan does have its own ambition and intention in defending Japan's interest by circumventing the U.S. influence and control. Japan owns a relatively small size of population (around 126 million) and of territory (about 377835 square kilometers), yet economically it has been an influential country. For a long period of time in history, Japan had been the second largest economy in the world, and now still remains as the third largest one. Unsurprisingly, Japan would tend to rely on its economic influence as a leverage to offset the shortcomings in the country's defence capacity.

In order to make itself more like a "normal state", during the second half of the 20th century, Japan had made enormous efforts in developing the country's capacity from a wide variety of aspects. Great progress had been made, in particular, in the economic sphere. Through actively participating in the process of building and promoting regional and global networks, mechanisms, and institutions, Japan had successfully managed to expand or diversify its economic partners. Generally, since the late 1990s, Japan has been gradually less influenced by the U.S. economic pressure.

There were some examples to be able to prove that the multilateral frameworks can be effective in helping build Japan's confidence in dealing with the U.S. pressure. For instance, in 1995, Japan took a counter-measure through the system of the World Trade Organization (WTO) in challenging a U.S. complaint against Japan in relation to the sale of autos and auto parts. Though the two countries finally decided to settle this matter outside the WTO, yet that was the first time for Japan to resist the U.S. demand.[13] Therefore, the settlement of that dispute carried an extraordinary meaning for Japan, as since then, instead of constantly making concessions in facing the U.S. pressure, Japan has found another means to better meet Japan's interests, which is to defend Japan's legitimate concerns through multilateral institutions and the international rule of law.

Then, in 1997, Japan won another case through the WTO in a dispute with the U.S. regarding the marketing of kodak and Fuji film in Japan.[14] Winning the case further consolidated Japan's confidence in challenging the United States. More crucially, it led to a major strategic shift of Japan from a broader sense toward managing its trade disputes with the United States. In William Cooper's words, "increased reliance on the WTO has reflected a major shift in Japan's strategy in dealing with the United States in trade."[15] Even though nowadays the WTO faces a lot of issues related to reform, for a certain period of time in history, Japan apparently had significantly benefited from the functioning of the WTO in helping safeguard Japan's legitimate interests.

In recent years, so far, with regard to Japan's relevance to a broad range of multilateral economic arrangements, Japan has been a member of the Regional Comprehensive Economic Partnership Agreement (RCEP). Japan also has engaged in discussions of a trilateral free trade agreement with South Korea and China, as well as in free trade talks with the European Union. Besides those, after the U.S. withdrew from the Trans-Pacific Partnership Agreement (TPP), Japan had taken a lead in forging a new multilateral economic framework, namely the Comprehensive and Progressive Agreement for Trans-Pacific Partnership (CPTPP), by including the parties having previously involved in the negotiations of the TPP into the CPTPP grouping. This new multilateral mechanism CPTPP entered into force on 30 December 2018. Further to the above, since early 2022, Japan has been engaged in the discussions with other partners based in the Indo-Pacific region toward jointly establishing a U.S.-led new economic framework. Finally, the Indo-Pacific Economic Framework for Prosperity (IPEF) was launched in Japan on 23 May 2022 by the U.S., Japan, and other 12 partners including Australia, Brunei Darussalam, Fiji, India, Indonesia, Republic of Korea, Malaysia, New Zealand, Philippines, Singapore, Thailand, and Vietnam.[16]

Obviously, Japan has been very active in pursuing and defending its economic interest. We can see that from the economic dimension, like other states, Japan has generally been able to act independently like a "Normal State", and has achieved both independence and inter-dependence in regional and global economic affairs.

Given the achievements made by Japan in the economic area over the past decades, apparently, engaging with the U.S. through multilateral arrangements rather than U.S.-Japan bilateral frameworks, especially in Japan's case, can make the country sense more certainties, as the multilateral arrangements have proved to be the effective means in better meeting Japan's economic interests by offsetting the economic pressure imposed by the U.S. in many occasions. Therefore, in the coming years, given the experiences accumulated by Japan in seeking independence and inter-dependence in the economic sphere, some measures and tactics ever applied will expect to be deployed in the security field as well, such as the kinds of measures related to continuously diversifying or expanding Japan's cooperation partners. Japan's security cooperation with its partners could range from joint peacekeeping operations, training, anti-piracy activities, humanitarian relief, to other kinds of exchanges aiming to strengthen capacity building etc. In addition, promoting the building and strengthening of networks, mechanisms, and institutions, and enhancing international rule of law and norms for facilitating quality cooperation will likely be the measures to be adopted by Japan as well in order to meet Japan's needs.

2.1 What Does Japan Aim to Achieve through Conducting Its Indo-Pacific Vision?

By bearing the above objectives in mind, the Indo-Pacific vision will be taken by Japan as the most effective strategy in the years ahead to serve Japan's needs in a broad range of aspects. To formulate and implement the strategy, the Japanese government has already invested great diplomatic efforts in bringing as many partners as possible to the Indo-Pacific region in order to expand the influence of the Indo-Pacific vision in both conceptual and practical terms.

From the Japanese perspective, holding Japan with the U.S. and other variety of partners together through the Indo-Pacific vision, on the one hand, could help Japan ease as much pressure as possible to be imposed by the U.S., in case the situation wouldn't be in Japan's favour. On the other hand, regardless of whether the U.S. influence in the Indo-Pacific region will be declining or growing in the decades ahead, it wouldn't generate great uncertainties to Japan. In addition to that, no matter whether China will be part of the Indo-Pacific vision or not in the future, the Indo-Pacific vision could also serve as a counter-balance to the possible challenges posed by China.

Overall, instead of being in a subordinate position, Japan aims to play a more dominant role in the Indo-Pacific region through framing and implementing the country's own Indo-Pacific vision. It is also intended to maintain a balance among all great players including the U.S., China, and other major powers, by doing so, to further raise Japan's influence, make Japan's interests well-protected, and generate more certainties for Japan's future.

As far as Japan manages to successfully implement its Indo-Pacific vision, even though Japan could still face a constraint in the country's defence capacity, it will not prevent Japan from being a greater player in regional and global affairs. Japan's economic size, diplomatic capacity, and technological advantage in a number of areas should also be a big plus for helping this country achieve the goal of becoming a more crucial player. To further extent, in line with its Indo-Pacific vision, Japan will likely become one of the poles in the international system, and be able to contribute to the forging of an Indo-Pacific order as well as of a new multi-polar world.

2.2 What Does the U.S. Want from Implementing the Indo-Pacific Strategy?

For the U.S. side, since former U.S. President Trump's tenure, the U.S. has already started to prioritize its interest in the Indo-Pacific region, and the Biden Administration has further consolidated the U.S. priority in this region. In February 2022, the U.S. government just released a report on the U.S. Indo-Pacific strategy. Against the backdrop that the U.S. would aim to sustain its influence in this region, it would certainly want to further augment Japan's role in helping implement the U.S. new strategy.

During former U.S. President Obama's term, alongside a major shift in the U.S. strategy toward Asia, the U.S. had held a higher expectation in Japan by then. As guided by the U.S. "pivot to Asia" strategy, Japan had made a lot of efforts in helping promote the implementation of the U.S. strategy in Southeast Asia.

After the Trump government took office, in line with the "American First" policy, the U.S. had generally downplayed the functioning of the U.S. traditional alliance tactics in helping achieve the U.S. strategic goals. The Trump government also emphasized the significance of freedom, openness, and shared values in the Indo-Pacific region, yet it mainly sought to meet the U.S. strategic interests in the Indo-Pacific region more in economic rather than in security terms.

With the U.S. President Biden coming to power, certain strategic and tactical measures ever applied by the Obama Administration including the U.S. alliance strategy were resumed. Then Japan was once again back to the central stage in the U.S. policy planning toward Asia.

Japan was expected by the U.S. side to help sustain the U.S. power in a variety of means including balancing the challenges to be probably posed by China.

To achieve its objectives, the U.S. would tend to deploy a wide range of bilateral and multilateral arrangements. From a bilateral sense, as usual, the U.S. would mainly seek to strengthen the U.S. bilateral relationships in various terms with its key allies in this region. From a multilateral dimension, in the economic area, so far, the U.S. hasn't expressed any interest in joining the Japan-led CPTPP as well as other economic pacts. Yet, the Biden government, since the beginning of 2022, has announced a series of plans related to the development of the U.S.-initiated economic framework, the IPEF, which, as a crucial part of the U.S. overall Indo-Pacific strategy, was set to serve as a guideline for the U.S. engagements with its allies and other various partners particularly in the economic field in the years ahead. The new economic initiative also reflected the U.S. intention to set the standards for the making of new rules in order to better meet the U.S. strategic interests in the region.

More specifically regarding the IPEF, it encompasses four pillars: "Trade; Supply Chains; Clean Energy, Decarbonization and Infrastructure; and Tax and Anti-corruption."[17] This new economic framework is more flexible; and the IPEF partners are free to choose which pillar(s) they would want to join. According to the information released by the Office of the United States Trade Representative (USTR) on 23 September, at the current stage, the trade pillar consists of 13 partners; and India is not among the list of partners for trade negotiations.[18]

The USTR on the same day also announced the U.S. negotiating goals and focused areas for the trade pillar - the general objective of the trade pillar was set to jointly achieve long-term prosperity in the Indo-Pacific region and also in the United States through building "high-standard, inclusive, free, and fair-trade commitments", as well as through generating "new and creative approaches" to help facilitate "trade and technology cooperation" among member countries; meanwhile, the IPEF's trade pillar would prioritize negotiations on these areas of issues: "labour, environment, digital economy, trade facilitation, agriculture, competition policy, transparency and good regulatory practices, inclusivity, and technical assistance and economic cooperation."[19]

The U.S. officials announced that the IPEF is different from a traditional free trade agreement, yet specifically for the trade pillar of this new framework, it is assumed that there will be a lot of similarities in the negotiation process between a traditional free trade agreement and the IPEF's trade pillar in terms of the relevant standards-setting, commitments of member countries, competition policy, regulatory practices, and others etc.

The purpose of implementing the IPEF is supposed to mutually meet a balanced interest among the negotiating partners and beyond. The U.S. and a diverse range of partners have jointly set the basic structures of the new framework. Regarding how the IPEF could be implemented, and how its members would proceed the negotiations and respond to each other's requests in the coming number of steps, as well as how likely other important actors based in the Indo-Pacific region would respond to the IPEF, we'll have to wait and see in the years to come.

As for the U.S. plan in the security area, from a multilateral sense, the U.S. would tend to rely on the Quadrilateral Security Dialogue (QUAD) and the Australia-United Kingdom-United States Trilateral Partnership (AUKUS) to help forge and implement the U.S. security policy agenda. Besides that, the U.S. would seek to form connections between the U.S.-led mechanisms and other various regional initiatives focusing on dealing with regional security issues.

The relevant initiatives led by the U.S. such as the AUKUS and the IPEF etc. are currently in the early stage of development. In the years ahead, as usual, the U.S. would want Japan to take more responsibilities in helping strengthen the capacity of a range of U.S.-led initiatives or frameworks, and in implementing the Indo-Pacific strategy as a whole. Then, how likely would the U.S.-Japan bilateral engagements be evolving in the years to come?

2.3 The Possible Scenarios of the U.S.-Japan Bilateral Relations under the Context of Carrying Out the Indo-Pacific Strategy

The Japanese government attaches great significance to its Indo-Pacific vision, which is different from the previous strategies launched by Japan. Japan has invested great diplomatic efforts in persuading a number of world leaders to back this initiative. Japan expected the Indo-

Pacific vision to be able to exert a global influence, by relying on which, to help Japan achieve strategic autonomy as maximally as it can. The Indo-Pacific vision is taken by the Japanese government as a public good to meet the interests of the countries in the Indo-Pacific region and beyond.

Therefore, under these circumstances, the implementation of the Indo-pacific strategy might lead to at least four possibilities in terms of its relevance to the likely development of the U.S.-Japan bilateral relations, one of which would be that it will be processed mostly in line with Japan's design and interest; in that case, there will be a likelihood for Japan to become one of the poles in a new multi-polar international system.

The second possibility would be that, alongside the growing role of Japan in the Indo-Pacific, frictions between the U.S. and Japan might emerge, just like the disputes ever happened between the two countries in the economic and trade area years ago. The root cause of the possible frictions would lie in the diverse strategic objectives between the two countries - Japan expects to achieve strategic autonomy as more possibly as this country would manage through carrying out its Indo-Pacific vision, while the increasing strategic autonomy of Japan, from the U.S. perspective, also means a diminishing influence of the U.S. over Japan. Therefore, how the two countries could manage the possible frictions in the process of implementing the Indo-Pacific strategy will significantly affect the status of the U.S. and of Japan in the region. It might be ended in two scenarios - either Japan would finally accede to the U.S. pressure, or Japan may choose to align more closely with other major players like India, China, or some influential European countries etc.

The third one could be that, without major struggles to take place between Japan and the U.S., as usual, Japan would play a subordinate role in proceeding the Indo-Pacific agenda, and act as part of the U.S.-led coalition or alliance in dealing with China. This scenario would more likely face a consequence of failure just like that the U.S. "Pivot to Asia" strategy ever faced years ago. The countries in the Indo-Pacific region as well as elsewhere are getting more cautious about the repercussions of taking sides between great powers. Any kinds of big conflicts in the Indo-Pacific would not be in their interests, given that the countries based in this region have generally benefited from a relatively stable and peaceful environment over the past few decades.

The fourth one could be that the implementation of the Indo-Pacific strategy might lead to a situation that the major powers including the U.S., China, India, Japan, and others could manage to find ways to peacefully coexist. This should be the most ideal scenario.

In the process of framing and implementing the Indo-Pacific strategy, apart from the possible outcomes led by the U.S.-Japan engagement, other number of factors - such as whether China would participate in it or not, and how possibly the implementation of the Indo-Pacific strategy would affect China-Japan or China-U.S. relations etc. - would also likely have big impacts on the forging and implementation of the Indo-Pacific agenda in the next steps. Furthermore, the positions held by India, Southeast Asian countries, and other powers are also of very significance in affecting the outcomes of this initiative. The following part of this piece would mainly focus on understanding how the China factor would possibly affect the outcomes of the Indo-Pacific strategy.

3. The United States, China, and Japan on the Indo-Pacific Strategy

3.1 A Brief Review of China-Japan Bilateral Cooperation in Trade, Investment, Tourism, and Security

Since China and Japan established diplomatic relations in 1972, the two countries have managed to develop a generally steady bilateral relationship - no serious conflict has taken place between them over the past years, with a close economic linkage while a relatively cold political relationship. For a certain period of time, China had ever been a main destination of Japan's official development assistance. Since the late 1990s and the beginning of the 21st century, especially with China's entry into the WTO, China in a relatively short period of time had grown to one of the major economic entities in the world, which made Japan sense the pressure, and further motivated Japan to compete with China for regional leadership in the economic sphere.

Meanwhile, alongside the U.S. strategic adjustment and the deepening of the U.S.-Japan cooperation in defence and security, China-Japan bilateral ties had so far undergone a few rounds of serious fluctuations roughly starting from the mid-2000s to the end of the U.S. "Pivot to Asia" strategy. A series of political frictions such as the former Japanese leadership's visit to the Yasukuni Shrine, Japan's revision of its textbook, and then Japanese government's intent to nationalize the disputed Diaoyu islands in 2012 etc. led to the discontent of the Chinese public to Japan and resulted in strong anti-Japan protests across many cities in China.[20] As a consequence, the normal economic activities in relation to trade, investments, and tourism between the two countries had been affected - China-Japan two-way trade was down from $345 billion in 2011 to $270 billion in 2016.[21]

With the U.S. "Rebalance of Asia" strategy coming to an end, the tension between China and Japan had been eased, and the figures in trade and investment had returned to a steady level within a short period of time. China-Japan trade, after having experienced a downward pressure driven by the strategic adjustment of both the U.S. and Japan during 2011-2016, reached more than $350 billion in 2018,[22] and further increased to $372.1 billion in 2021,[23] even though the global economy has been facing a recession caused by the COVID-19 pandemic since early 2020. Chinese visitors to Japan topped slightly less than 8.4 million in the same year, making China the top source of all foreign visitors to Japan.[24] With regard to the amount of Japan's foreign direct investment (FDI) in China, apart from the short period of 2002-2005 and of 2010-2013, Japan's FDI flowing to China over the years has generally maintained a steady number ranging between $35 billion and $40 billion annually.[25]

In recent years, Japanese policy-makers have intended to increase the share of Japan's investments in other parts of the world, in particular, southeast Asia. Nevertheless, China still remains as a major destination for Japanese foreign investments. Generally, the range of frictions caused by the policy adjustment of both Japan and the U.S. didn't alter the fundamentals of China-Japan economic connectivity. China is still of the largest trading partner of Japan.

With regard to security collaboration between two countries, China appeared to be more cautious and reluctant toward security cooperation with Japan, due to the historical issue between the two countries as well as the disputes of them in the East China Sea. In addition, the U.S.-Japan security treaty alliance and Japan's heavy reliance on the U.S. for national defence are assumed to have played a role also in narrowing down the possibility of China-Japan security cooperation.

However, there have been some special occasions for security collaboration between the two nations over the past few years. For instance, a Japanese private nongovernmental organization, named Sasakawa Foundation, ever facilitated exchanges for officers from the Japan Self-Defence Forces (SDF) and the People's Liberation Army (PLA) in February 2018.[26] In addition to that, following Chinese Premier Li Keqiang's official visit to Japan in May 2018, and thereafter former Japanese Prime Minister Shinzo Abe's visit to China in October the same year, China-Japan bilateral relations further warmed up a bit in 2018. Apart from a set of agreements reached between the two nations in the economic area, China and Japan had also managed to make a new breakthrough in security cooperation, as reflected by the fact that, after having been in negotiation for more than a decade, the two countries finally signed an agreement on Maritime and Aerial Communication Mechanism in May 2018.[27]

The above agreement can be traced to an earlier engagement on security between the two countries back in 2008. By then, for security concerns, Japan proposed to jointly form a China-Japan "military crisis management mechanism", which was in principle agreed by China the same year.[28] Nevertheless, due to a number of reasons obviously including the fluctuations of the external environment in the region and also of China-Japan diplomatic relations, the signing of a China-Japan agreement concerning security issues had been delayed for about a decade.

The China-Japan Maritime and Aerial Communication Mechanism, according to the *Defence of Japan 2018 White Paper*, mainly consisted of the following three components: "first, annual and expert meetings between the two countries' defence authorities; second, a hotline between Japanese and Chinese defence authorities; and third, on scene communication measures between vessels and aircraft of the SDF and the PLA."[29]

3.2 Japan's Indo-Pacific Vision & the Indo-Pacific Strategy of the United States - A Comparison

Against the background of the changing regional and global environment, both Japan and the United States have set up their Indo-Pacific agendas. Japan has laid out three key pillars in Japan's Indo-

Pacific vision. The first pillar covers the elements of rule of law, freedom of navigation and overflight, and free trade.[30] Via the Indo-Pacific vision, Japan expressed its intention to build connectivity with the Middle Eastern and African regions, and to help share the successful experiences gathered by the Association of Southeast Asian Nations (ASEAN) in a broad range of areas including development to these two regions.[31] By doing so, on the one hand, the influence of the Indo-Pacific vision can be expanded to other regions; on the other hand, Japan also expected, through developing close connections with these two regions, to help secure Japan's energy security as well as to further explore the opportunities of the African continent. By bearing these purposes in mind, Japan in the first pillar of its Indo-Pacific vision highlighted the significance of protecting the sea lanes, of guaranteeing freedom of navigation and overflight, and of promoting free trade, in line with the rule of law.

The second pillar of Japan's Indo-Pacific vision is designed to achieve common economic prosperity in the Indo-Pacific region through building connectivity, developing quality infrastructure projects, promoting investments, and improving business environment.[32]

The third pillar of it aims to achieve peace and stability in the Indo-Pacific region through increasing resilience and strengthening capacity building including promoting maritime law enforcement and maritime domain awareness, enhancing cooperation in humanitarian assistance and disaster relief, and promoting collaboration in anti-piracy, and counter-terrorism etc.[33]

There are similarities between the U.S. and Japan in their Indo-Pacific agendas such as the objectives related to promoting freedom of navigation, building connectivity, achieving economic prosperity, and improving capacity building etc. Nevertheless, from a strategic perspective by taking into account the national interests of each of them, differences between them remain very apparently.

For Japan, the Indo-Pacific agenda is set to help secure strategic autonomy of Japan and generate more certainties for the country's future. In addition to that, energy security is of a more crucial issue for Japan than for the U.S.. Hence, Japan highlighted the significance of the connectivity between Japan and the Middle East. Meanwhile, by promoting collaboration with the countries outside the Indo-Pacific region, Japan would seek to expand the influence of its Indo-Pacific agenda. Under Japan's Indo-Pacific vision, it appears that the strategic regions cover East Asia, Southeast Asia, South Asia, Middle East, and Africa.

For the U.S., as shown in a report on the Indo-Pacific Strategy released by the U.S. government on February 2022, the strategic regions under the U.S. Indo-Pacific agenda mainly encompass Northeast Asia, Southeast Asia, South Asia, and the Oceanian including the Pacific Islands.[34] From a geographic perspective, the countries based in these regions are close neighbours of China. Therefore, the designing of the U.S. Indo-Pacific strategy would mostly target China.

Through implementing its Indo-Pacific agenda, the U.S. aims to advance the country's interest and to deal with its competition with China by strengthening the Indo-Pacific region together with the U.S. allies and partners, as the U.S. revealed in the Indo-Pacific framework that "Our collective efforts over the next decade will determine whether the PRC succeeds in transforming the rules and norms that have benefited the Indo-Pacific and the world. ... Our objective is not to change the PRC but to shape the strategic environment in which it operates, building a balance of influence in the world that is maximally favourable to the United States, our allies, and partners, and the interest and values we share."[35] Meanwhile, in the Indo-Pacific framework, the U.S. also expressed its intention to handle the competition with China responsibly, and to seek to cooperate with China in areas like climate change and nonproliferation.[36]

From the above, we can see that the U.S. new strategy has shifted away from aiming to change China to purposely altering the strategic environment in which China operates. By doing so, the U.S. expects to achieve the outcome that China doesn't appear to have more alternative options apart from following the rules, norms, and standards set by the U.S. To achieve these, the U.S. will plan to invest in the Indo-Pacific region in both material and non-material terms, though it appears that the U.S. will mostly be ready to achieve its goals through injecting greater diplomatic efforts, which could range from enhancing the U.S. bilateral and multilateral relationships with its allies and partners, to strengthening the capacity of regional countries from a variety of aspects such as improving their capacity in maritime law enforcement, cyber protection, management of health security, and climate adaption etc., as well as to investing in deepening cooperation in the fields related to supply hains, infrastructure, and joint technology development etc.[37]

More specifically regarding the above, for instance, in line with the action plans of the U.S. Indo-Pacific agenda for improving the capacity of Southeast Asian countries, the U.S. would invest more in deepening the U.S.-ASEAN ties including allocating more than $100 million in new U.S.-ASEAN initiatives.[38]

Overall, strengthening the capacity of the countries in the Indo-Pacific region will be one of the key measures for the U.S. to achieve its goals set under the country's Indo-Pacific agenda. Then, how likely will the U.S. be able to reach the outcomes as it designed and expected under its Indo-Pacific strategy?

3.3 China's Relevance to the Possible Outcomes of Implementing the Indo-Pacific Strategy

Currently, the relevant new frameworks and measures for the U.S.-Indo pacific agenda are still in the early stage of planning. The IPEF is the first multilateral trade agreement set by the U.S. in the Indo-Pacific region. As already analysed in the previous part, the purpose of initiating this new economic framework is to enable the U.S. to take a new lead in setting rules and standards in core economic issue areas covered by this framework, and to isolate China by changing the strategic environment in which China works. However, it would be unrealistic to isolate China from and cut China's connections with a wide variety of established regional and global networks and mechanisms, as far as the relevant mechanisms/networks/initiatives keep functioning to be able to serve the interests of the concerned parties beyond.

With regard to the specifically focused areas of the IPEF such as improving the supply chain resilience, it is very much related to the capacity and convenience in producing, trading, and distributing various kinds of goods and services with higher quality and competitive prices at the regional and global markets. Using disrupting means to handle this issue would only damage the regional and global production and supply chains as a whole. As for decarbonization and clean development, China currently is a large emitter, China's commitment to decarbonization would significantly contribute to the global efforts in addressing climate challenges. The U.S., as a large emitter as well, has been seeking to cooperate with China in this field over the past years. China-U.S. cooperation in the climate area in substantial terms would be very necessary and can serve as a good example for other countries to follow a clean development path as well in the long-term future. Regarding infrastructure development, many developing countries in the Indo-Pacific region and beyond urgently need quality infrastructure to facilitate the development of their nations. In line with their interests and needs, these countries should be free to choose which partners to cooperate with in this area.

Another issue in relation to the IPEF is that, according to the relevant information released so far, it may not be a binding agreement. If it is not binding, the issue of whether the U.S. will be able to fulfill its commitments should be put into question. Even if the U.S. government manages to make it a binding agreement, given the records of the U.S. withdrawing from a number of agreements or commitments in the past, whether the U.S. can fulfill its obligations should be doubted by the stakeholders as well. After all, framing and implementing the IPEF in the Indo-Pacific region would likely face a lot of uncertainties and possibilities. The most crucial concern for the IPEF partners in the future will be that whether the IPEF would be able to deliver more tangible outcomes.

Now, against the background that both the U.S. and Japan have set up their Indo-Pacific agendas, for the general trend of China-Japan bilateral collaboration in the years ahead, economic and trade cooperation will likely continue to be a crucial force in driving the overall China-Japan bilateral relations. As usual, apart from China-Japan bilateral engagement, the two will also tend to deal with each other through a broad range of multilateral forums/mechanism/institutions. Both countries are the members of the G20 and of the RCEP. China is currently in the process of applying for the membership of the CPTPP.

The general picture of Japan-China engagement concerning economic and trade issues in the foreseeable future will not likely undergo great fluctuations. For other areas of cooperation between the two countries such as security, apart from what the two nations have already achieved, China and Japan could seek the possibility of deepening or expanding their collaboration in this realm. For instance, the two countries may explore the opportunities of jointly conducting peacekeeping operations, anti-piracy activities, or humanitarian relief actions etc. Furthermore, the two sides could seek the likelihood of cooperating on other range of issues such as joint infrastructure projects in third party countries.

Generally, the steady engagement between China and Japan either through bilateral arrangements or through multilateral frameworks would be conducive to the implementation of Japan's Indo-Pacific vision. To further extent, Japan's Indo-Pacific vision would likely face more certainties.

For the version of the U.S. overall Indo-Pacific strategy, as already discussed in the previous part of this study, enhancing the U.S. values, seeking to deepen cooperation with the countries, institutions, and mechanisms in the Indo-Pacific region, strengthening the capability of the U.S.-led initiatives, as well as improving the capacity of certain Indo-Pacific countries in managing a wide variety of tasks, risks, and challenges will be the primary means to be deployed by the U.S. in implementing its Indo-Pacific strategy.

With regard to China-U.S. interactions on economic and trade issues, so far, the U.S. in the IPEF has expressed its intention to invite other partners based in the Indo-Pacific region to join the U.S.-initiated framework. At the current stage, it is still early to tell whether China would consider joining it or not, or how likely China would tend to engage with the U.S. over the implementation of this new economic framework and of the U.S. Indo-Pacific strategy as a whole in the next steps.

Overall, regardless of how the Indo-Pacific strategy will be further framed and implemented, and of whether the U.S. will be able to achieve the outcomes as it designed and expected through carrying out its Indo-Pacific agenda, the U.S. will not give up its interest in the Indo-Pacific region in the decades ahead, given that there will be full of greater potentials in various terms in the Indo-Pacific region from a long-term perspective. According to the information cited from the White House website, "with 60% of the world's population, the Indo-Pacific is projected to be the largest contributor to global growth over the next 30 years."[39]

At the current stage, it appears that the U.S. intends to deal with China by applying certain traditional tactics ever deployed by the great powers in history. The U.S. may adjust its strategies and methods from time to time in the process of further framing and implementing its Indo-Pacific agenda; and in a long-term future, there might be a possibility that China, the U.S., and other major powers would be able to find more peaceful, effective, and balanced means in managing their relations. Under those circumstances, the core stakeholders would enjoy a happy ending together. On the contrary, then the most likely outcome would be that, instead of being able to isolate China from a wide range of regional and global networks and mechanisms, the U.S. itself would risk being isolated, and the U.S. status and power, in particular, the country's soft power would risk further declining, alongside the growing role of other major powers/entities in the region such as India, Japan, and ASEAN etc.

Conclusion

This chapter has mainly assessed how the implementation of the Indo-Pacific strategy could possibly impact on the positions of the three major powers in the Indo-Pacific region, the U.S., Japan, and China, as well as whether and how the China factor could affect the outcomes of the U.S. Indo-Pacific strategy and of Japan's Indo-Pacific vision.

In the first part, it has given a brief overview of the U.S.-Japan bilateral collaboration on economic, trade, and security issues. For a long period of time after the end of WWII, Japan had been subject to the great pressure of the United States in these areas. With the great efforts made by Japan as well as with the changing geo-economic and geo-political situation in the Asia Pacific, by late 1990s, Japan had managed to achieve economic strategic autonomy by circumventing the U.S. control, while in the security realm, Japan's position so far hasn't changed dramatically. Nevertheless, the constraint in Japan's defence capacity hasn't prevented this country from growing to an economically and technologically influential power.

The second part of it has intended to understand the mentality of the U.S.-Japan collaboration in the past as well as in the future under the great context of framing and implementing the Indo-Pacific agenda. Both countries obviously hold a complicated mentality to each other. The U.S. main concern is to ally with Japan but not to lose control over Japan's influence in the Indo-Pacific region and beyond; while Japan's primary goal is to achieve strategic autonomy as maximally as it can in order to meet Japan's ambition and to better serve the country's national interest. Therefore, there are certain differences to remain, more from a strategic perspective, between the U.S. and Japan. Under this circumstance, this piece assumed a point that the U.S.-Japan engagements would likely have a significant impact on the possible shaping of an Indo-Pacific order.

The third part of this study has assessed how the China factor could affect the outcomes of the Indo-Pacific strategy. It would generally conclude a point that whether China will be part of the U.S.-initiated Indo-Pacific strategy or of the Japan-launched Indo-Pacific vision, the implementation of the Indo-Pacific agenda wouldn't fundamentally change China's connections with a broad variety of regional and global networks and mechanisms, mostly because the networks and frameworks facilitated under the Indo-Pacific strategy cannot be completely separated from China-involved networks, forums, or mechanisms. In this regard, even if China wouldn't clearly demonstrate its participation in the Indo-Pacific strategy, the connection - which could be either in a direct way or in an indirect way - between China and the Indo-Pacific strategy cannot be denied.

In the process of framing and implementing the Indo-Pacific agenda, even though the measures to be applied by the U.S. in the years ahead will likely have some similarities with the tactics and means deployed by the U.S. in the past, against the backdrop of the changing geo-economic and geo-political conditions, the implementation of the Indo-Pacific strategy could lead to a number of possibilities in a long run. That means that there could be a possibility for China, Japan, and the U.S. to engage with each other more openly and closely through the Indo-Pacific agenda. If this is the case, the implementation of the Indo-Pacific strategy will likely generate more certainties for the development of the trilateral relations of the U.S., China, and Japan, as well as for the region and the world.

Notes

1. Kuo Yujen, "Japan's Roles in the Indo-Pacific Strategy", *Prospect Journal,* NO.19:29, https://www.pf.org.tw/files/6236/8B3BC62D-6F19-4E23-8D96-3BBC3042464F

2. Cooper H. William, "U.S.-Japan Economic Relations: Significance, Prospects, and Policy Options", *Congressional Research Service,* 18

February 2014.

3. Dong Yan and Xu Qiyuan, "Staying the Course of Deepening Reform and Opening-up in Facing the U.S.-China Trade War", P139, Shanghai Pushan Foundation, February 2020.

4. Ibid.

5. Cooper H. William, "U.S.-Japan Economic Relations: Significance, Prospects, and Policy Options", *Congressional Research Service*, 18 February 2014.

6. Ibid.

7. Ibid.

8. Hoff Rachel, "Next Steps for U.S.-Japan Security Cooperation", *SASAKAWA USA.*

9. Ibid.

10. Ibid.

11. Ibid.

12. Chiang Min-Hua, "Contemporary China-Japan Relations: the Politically Driven Economic Linkage", *East Asia (2019),* 36:285, Springer.

13. Cooper H. William, "U.S.-Japan Economic Relations: Significance, Prospects, and Policy Options", *Congressional Research Service*, 18 February 2014.

14. Ibid.

15. Ibid, P19.

16. Office of the United States Trade Representative, "The Indo-Pacific Economic Framework for Prosperity: Biden-Harris Administration's Negotiating Goals for the Connected Economy (Trade) Pillar", 23 September2022,https://ustr.gov/about-us/policy-offices/press-office/ press-releases/2022/september/indo-pacific-economic-framework- prosperity-biden-harris-administrations-negotiating-goals-connected

17. Ibid.

18. Ibid.

19. Ibid.

20. Chiang Min-Hua, "Contemporary China-Japan Relations: the Politically Driven Economic Linkage", *East Asia (2019),* 36:285, Springer.

21. Ibid.

22. Harold W. Scoh, "Regional Responses to U.S.-China Competition in the Indo-Pacific", *RAND,* 2020.

23. Data related to two-way trade between China and Japan in 2021 was cited from the Ministry of Foreign Affairs of Japan, https://www.mofa.go.jp/

region/asia-paci/china/data.html
24. Harold W. Scoh, "Regional Responses to U.S.-China Competition in the Indo-Pacific", *RAND,* 2020.
25. Ibid, P11.
26. Ibid.
27. Ibid.
28. Ibid, P23.
29. Cited from Harold W. Scoh, "Regional Responses to U.S.-China Competition in the Indo-Pacific", *RAND,* 2020, P23.
30. Mission of Japan to ASEAN, "A New Foreign Policy Strategy: 'A free and open Indo-Pacific Strategy'", https://www.asean.emb-j apan.go.jp/files/000352880.pdf
31. Ibid.
32. Ibid.
33. Ibid.
34. The White House, "Indo-Pacific Strategy of the United States", 11 February 2022, https://www.whitehouse.gov/wp-content/uploads/ 2022 /02/U.S.-Indo-Pacific-Strategy.pdf
35. Ibid.
36. Ibid.
37. Ibid.
38. Ibid.
39. The White House, "FACT SHEET: In Asia, President Biden and A Dozen Indo-Pacific Partners Launch the Indo-Pacific Economic Framework for Prosperity", 23 May 2022, https://www.whitehouse.gov/briefing-room/statements-releases/2022/05/23/fact-sheet-in-asia-president-biden-and-a-dozen-indo-pacific-partners-launch-the-indo-pacific-economic-framework-for-prosperity/

CHAPTER 3

The Ukraine Crisis & the Prospect of Forging A New European Order and beyond

The Russia-Ukraine conflict started since 24 February 2022 has drawn enormous global attention. Following the eruption of the conflict, the U.S. and its allies have launched many rounds of severe sanctions against Russia, which, apart from visa bans and asset freezes, mainly targeted Russia's financial, energy, defence, and transportation sectors. To this stage, the main parties having a relevance to the Ukrainian crisis including the U.S., Russia, the European Union, and Ukraine have suffered various degrees of losses. As far as the fighting on the ground cannot be stopped, more devastating consequences would emerge from occasion to occasion.

The current crisis once again reminded people of the tragedies happened in Ukraine eight to nine years ago as a result of the first Ukraine crisis. At a later stage of the first crisis, following the signing of the Minsk-2 Agreement, the controversies between Russia and Ukraine and between the Ukrainian authority and the anti-Ukrainian government forces in the Donbas region, before the eruption of the second Ukraine crisis, had been frozen for about seven years.

The failure in implementing the two Minsk Agreements, alongside the escalation of other range of conflicting interests between Russia and the U.S.-led west, had drove the old controversies between Russia and

Ukraine to float up to the surface again. The intensification of all these conflicting matters finally culminated in the second Ukraine crisis.

In contrast to the first Ukraine crisis, the current one appears to be more complicated to handle, and it would likely generate broad implications beyond the European continent, given that the world over the past eight years has been undergoing a lot of changes including the leadership changes of major European powers, of Ukraine, and also of the U.S., the social and economic repercussions led by the COVID-19 pandemic across the world, and more crucially the adjustment of the U.S. strategies toward Europe and Asia.

Against the background that the United States, which has long been involved in the internal and external affairs of Ukraine, is planning to deepen the implementation of its Indo-Pacific strategy; and that the U.S. has shown its intention to align its strategies toward Europe and Asia together in order to better serve a broader and long-term interest of the United States.

Under these circumstances, the settlement of the Ukraine crisis would likely carry a more significant meaning for both the U.S. and the major powers in Europe and Asia. There is a need to observe how the U.S. would tend to link what have been happening in Europe including the Russia-Ukraine conflict with what the U.S. would plan to carry out in the Indo-Pacific region, and in the meantime how other main actors would act in response to the implementation of the U.S. strategies in the years ahead, due to that the outcomes of the interactions of various factors will likely decide how the future regional and world order would be like.

The purpose of this research is to examine the implications of the Ukraine crisis to the four main parties, the U.S., Russia, the EU, and Ukraine in social, economic, and strategic terms, then based on the understanding of which, to foresee how likely the settlement of the Ukraine crisis could affect the possible forging of a new European order and beyond.

To serve this research objective, this chapter will begin by exploring in details of the origins of the Ukraine crisis. Then it will investigate and analyse the evolution of Russia's relations with the U.S.-led west since the end of the Cold War in 1991. Further the project will assess the possible social, economic, and strategic implications of the Ukraine crisis to the major parties concerned. Finally, based on the understanding and analysis of the major parties' strategic interests, this project will tend to explore whether there could be any possible means not only for ending the current Ukraine crisis, but also for better serving a long-term interest of the parties concerned. The last part will also attempt to foresee the relevance of the management of the Ukraine crisis to the possible shaping of a new European order and beyond.

1. What Caused the Ukraine Crisis?

About nine years have passed since the eruption of the first Ukraine crisis. What had happened throughout the first Ukraine crisis might still be occasionally lingering around the minds of some people who had been affected by it. A series of small incidents resulted in the breaking out of the first Ukraine crisis. Initially, as welcomed and supported by certain western countries, a peaceful demonstration in the Maidan Square in Kyiv in November 2013 took place; and meanwhile a series of protests also occurred in other few cities of Ukraine. The protesters were motivated by their discontent with the Ukrainian Yanukovych government's failure to sign an Association Agreement (AA), which consisted of a free trade agreement, with the European Union. Then, due to the Yanukovych government's handling of the protests in forceful means, the nature of the demonstrations changed from opposing the government's failure to sign the AA to opposing the government's disrespect of the dignity of the Ukrainians. Further, following the government's crackdown of the protests in the Maidan Spare, which led to the death of more than 100 protesters, the situation became more uncontrollable and chaotic. The demonstrators started to occupy the government buildings. Yanukovych and his supporters fled Ukraine. On 27 February 2014, the Ukrainian parliament authorized an interim government to handle the situation.[1]

With the collapse of the Yanukovych government, in response to the chaotic situation in Ukraine, Russia immediately intervened by sending forces to take control of Crimea. In March 2014, a referendum was held in Crimea, with a 83% turnout rate, and 96% of the votes approving to join Russia. On 18 March 2014, Crimea officially became a permanent part of Russia.[2]

In the meantime, anti-Ukrainian government riots also broke out in the eastern region of Ukraine. They further led to a full-scale conflict between the separatists and the Ukrainian government forces.[3]

Then in response to the eruption of the Ukraine crisis, the U.S. and the European countries showed a different attitude toward Russia at the very early stage - apart from condemnation, the U.S. took the lead in sanctioning Russia and also urged the European countries to do the same; while the Europeans were generally reluctant to use sanctions against Russia, due to their closer economic linkage with Russia. Nevertheless, as a result of mistakenly shooting down the Malaysia Airlines flight MH17, which was assumed by many having a connection to Russia-backed forces, 298 passengers on board, most of whom were EU citizens, died. The accident altered the European countries' position toward Russia. The EU sanctions on Russia were then quickly followed through.[4]

Later on, under the mediation of then French President Francois Hollande and German Chancellor Angela Merkel, the four parties including Russia, Ukraine, France, and Germany together signed the Minsk-1 agreement in September 2014, and later the Minsk-2 agreement in February 2015. The most crucial part of the Minsk agreement was about the future status of the two territorial areas in the Donbas region, Luhansk and Donetsk. In accordance to the agreement, the two areas would be authorized a special autonomous status, which would be written into the Ukrainian Constitution. In addition to that, the individuals in the Donbas region having ever participated in the anti-government activities would be free of charge and punishment by the Ukrainian government.[5]

At a later stage, the western countries had urged both Ukraine and Russia to fulfill their obligations stated in the Minsk agreement. In a meeting with then Ukrainian President Poroshenko in February 2016, the foreign ministers of France and Germany urged the Ukrainian side to make constitutional amendment by upholding its part of the Minsk agreement. In the same month, the foreign minister of Denmark also pressed Ukraine to commit its part of the Minsk agreement, otherwise, Ukraine might risk losing the support of the EU to use sanctions against Russia.[6] Meanwhile, The EU also set a condition for Russia that only did Russia take steps to implement the Minsk agreement and ease the tension in the eastern region of Ukraine, the EU sanctions on Russia could be gradually lifted.[7]

Yet, the implementation of the Minsk agreement had been trapped in a stalemate. For the Ukrainian side, the Poroshenko government wasn't prepared to implement the agreement, and indicated that it was "politically unpalatable" to the country.[8] Under the Zelensky government, Ukraine didn't seem to be ready to meet Ukraine's commitments as well.

More recently, as uncovered by former German Chancellor Angela Merkel that the Minsk agreement was supposed to mainly serve a purpose of buying Ukraine more time for the country to build a stronger military.[9] This revelation apparently told that, back in 2014 and 2015, the then Ukrainian authority signed two Minsk agreements that the country had never been prepared to fulfil. In this regard, while still recognizing Ukraine as a victim of Russia's special military operation, the fact revealed by Mrs. Merkel can also make the Russian side affirm the legitimacy of its preemptive military operation against Ukraine.

Anyway, as the relevant sides have seen, as far as the Minsk agreement cannot be comprehensively implemented, apparently the frictions between Russia and Ukraine and between the Ukrainian authority and the anti-government forces in the eastern part of Ukraine cannot be properly settled; and peace in the Donbas region cannot be attained and sustained. Though the failure in implementing the Minsk agreement wasn't the root cause of the Ukraine crisis, it did play a crucial part in contributing to the breaking out of the second Ukraine crisis.

There are numerous factors having contributed to the eruption of the first and second Ukraine crisis, among which, the fundamental cause was the long-term rivalry between the U.S.-led west and Russia. More precisely, the origin of the Ukraine crisis was the continued implementation of the Cold War policy by the U.S. and some western countries toward Russia.

As generally believed, the Cold War ended in 1991 with the dissolution of the Soviet Union. In reality, it hasn't appeared to be over yet, as the polices carried out by the U.S. and certain western countries toward Russia since the 1990s, in comparison to their policies adopted roughly from the end of WWII to 1991, haven't fundamentally changed. After the disintegration of the Soviet Union, the Cold War seemed to have entered a new stage and been exhibited in a different form. We may name it as the Phase-2 Cold War.

A noticeable difference between Phase-1 and Phase-2 is that during the Phase-1 Cold War, the U.S. had mostly allied with the major

European powers to compete with the Soviet Union for sphere of influence; while throughout the period of the Phase-2 Cold War so far, apart from linking the U.S. strategies with its traditional allies, the U.S. has sought to ally with the former Soviet republics and the former Warsaw Pact members to balance Russia and to further narrow Russia's acting space through the expansion of NATO membership.

2. Evolution of Russia's Relations with the U.S.-led West: Continuity of the Cold War

The evolution of the Phase-2 Cold War can be roughly divided into three periods: from 1991 to the end of the 1990s, through the late 1990s to the early 2010s, and from the early 2010s to the current stage. Generally, the direction of the Phase-2 Cold War has been driven by the U.S., yet the U.S. and some of its European allies have had different policy priorities toward Russia. Therefore, the following part of this study will separately analyse how Russia's relations with the U.S. and with the EU have evolved respectively alongside their policies implemented throughout the three periods just mentioned.

2.1 Early 1990s - Late 1990s: from Warmness to Coldness

In the very early 1990s, the atmosphere in the western world was overwhelmed by the victory of the west and the failure of the Soviet Union. Both the western countries and Russia were in need to seek proper means to adapt to a new regional and international situation by interacting with various new partners.

For the west, the top priority was to transform Russia and other former Soviet republics into a number of capitalist democracies in line with the west-designed model. The west embraced the idea that the western model of governance, norms, and values could help transform Russia into a good partner, and make Russia be part of the western society ultimately.

For Russia, in the early days after the Phase-1 Cold War, it wasn't against the western model of democracy and free-market economy etc., and was hopeful of turning Russia into a strong, stable, and prosperous society by adapting to the western model and ideas.

Therefore, in the early 1990s, the west and Russia had managed to reach a series of common understandings within a very short period of time.

2.1.1 The U.S. and Russia in the 1990s

In the early days after the Cold War, the U.S. and Russia had striven to secure a convergence on a number of issues, which were considered strategically significant for the U.S., Russia, and Europe, including reducing strategic nuclear weapons, signing a multilateral treaty on conventional forces in Europe, negotiating the terms for the re-unification of Germany and also for the country's membership in NATO, as well as agreeing on a charter for European security and stability after the Cold War etc.[10] In addition to that, upon the first summit of then U.S. President Clinton and then Russian President Yeltsin, the two leaders pledged to develop a "new democratic partnership", and vowed to have a "robust engagement" between the two countries.[11]

Apart from the strategic and diplomatic consensus reached, with regard to the aspect of supporting Russia's domestic reforms, the U.S. had offered to provide Russia with economic and technical assistance. Much of the aid had been delivered under the guidance of the 1992 Freedom Support Act, conditioned with Russia's commitment to strengthening democratic governance, respecting human rights, and developing a free-market economy.[12]

However, the good momentum in the early 1990s toward developing a bright future relationship between the U.S. and Russia didn't last long. The first noticeable discrepancy between the two sides emerged as a result of, in Autumn 1993, the U.S. declaring to take NATO expansion as a "principal pillar" of its foreign policy in Europe, which was strongly opposed by Russia.[13]

From 1994 to 1997, the tension was further escalated due to a range of frictions subsequently occurred between the two countries including the U.S. opposition to the military campaign launched by Russia in dealing with the Chechnya separatists, and in the meantime Russia's opposition to the threat of NATO air strikes against Bosnian Serbs.[14] Then, the U.S. announcement of offering NATO membership to Poland, the Czech Republic, and Hungary in 1996 dragged Russia-U.S. relations further down.[15]

In addition to the above, with regard to Russia's domestic reforms, the advice offered by the U.S., instead of bringing prosperity and stability to Russia, had led to the dysfunction of the country's governance system, and turned Russia into a fertile soil for the growing of corruption and of oligarchs.

Overall, U.S.-Russia relations can be characterized by starting from warmness in the early 1990s to coldness in the late 1990s. From the series of policies taken by the U.S., Russia felt being deceived by the U.S., and believed that the U.S. had generally attempted to take advantage of Russia during the most difficult times of the country.

2.1.2 The Situation in Europe in the 1990s

Russia and the European countries in the 1990s had generally prioritized the economic aspect of their relations. Security issues had been relatively downplayed by both sides. The EU was in a main position in helping the transformation and reform process of Russia and of other former Soviet republics.

To facilitate the reform process, one of the most significant documents reached between Russia and the EU was the Partnership and Cooperation Agreement (PCA), which was signed in 1994 and came into force in 1997. The PCA mainly covered three areas: promoting economic and legal reform, facilitating Russia's compliance to international norms, and taking the economic aspect of Russia-EU relations as the number one priority.[16]

The PAC wouldn't be able to lead Russia to a member of the EU, mostly because, instead of being part of the EU, Russia would prefer to have a direct relationship with the EU based on equality and mutual respect.[17]

Obviously, in the early days after the Phase-1 Cold War, Russia wasn't particularly against the western model, norms, as well as European integration, yet Russia still highlighted the significance in keeping Russia's independent sovereign status in dealing with the EU. The PCA can be a contrast to the Association Agreement (AA) signed between the EU and other former eastern bloc states, as the AA would have the prospect of directing these states to attain a membership of the EU.[18]

The transformation process hadn't gone through smoothly. One of the common challenges faced by Russia and other newly independent states was the dysfunction of the domestic governance system. The transformation in some states had generated a "hybrid political system" mixed with democracy and autocracy.[19]

Although the political elites in the newly independent states did have the strong political will to proceed the relevant reforms, the reality was that both the government institutions and other various sectors within these countries hadn't been ready to adapt to a completely different political and economic system in a short-term. Under such circumstances, fast and forced transformation from a socialist planned economy to a capitalist market economy at an enormous scale and within a short period of time had only led to the disappointment of the EU, of Russia, and of other newly independent states.

2.2 Late 1990s - Early 2010s: Competing for Influence in the Post-Soviet Space

2.2.1 The EU and Russia: Striving to Formulate New Strategies and Policy Instruments

Following the failure in integrating Russia and other former Soviet republics into the European system throughout the 1990s, from the late 1990s, both the EU and these states had started to re-adjust their policy measures. The Period between the late 1990s and the early 2000s, alongside the new policy tools taken subsequently by the EU and Russia, had also marked the beginning for the two sides to compete for influence in the post-Soviet space.

In June 1999, after the EU Council issued a "Common Strategy of the EU toward Russia", Russia in response in October the same year also released a "Middle Term Strategy toward the EU", which was planned to be carried out through the period of 2000-2010.[20] Given the discrepancies Russia had experienced through the transformation process in the 1990s, the Middle-Term Strategy once again affirmed Russia's intent to keep its independent position in both domestic and foreign affairs by stating that "during the period covered by the strategy, neither Russian membership of the EU, nor formal association is on the agenda Russia must have the freedom and independence to determine its own domestic and foreign policy."[21] Besides that, for the prospect of developing a partnership with the EU, Russia took the EU as a very significant partner, and proposed, through the Middle Term Strategy, to form an "effective system of collective security" with its

European partners based on the principle of equality.[22]

During the late 1990s and the early 2010s, Russia had taken certain concrete moves in promoting institutional building, through which, to develop closer connectivity with the former Soviet republics, and to tie Russia's interest with theirs. The formation of the Eurasian Customs Union (ECU), which was later developed to the Eurasian Economic Union (EEU), can be a good example to prove Russia's planning in getting closer to the former Soviet republics.

Meanwhile, the EU had also created a series of foreign policy tools in managing its relations with Russia and with other eastern bloc states in order to expand the EU's role in the post-Soviet region. The series of foreign policy instruments developed by the EU from the late 1990s to the mid-2000s roughly consisted of the following:

The "EU Common Strategies for Russia and Ukraine", the "EU Special Representatives" which entitled the EU to act as a mediator in settling regional crisis, the "Police Missions" which allowed the EU to dispatch police missions to the Ukrainian-Moldovan border to help deal with illegal cross-border trade, the "European Neighbourhood Policy" which started to develop from 2002 and carried a special mission of promoting democracy and market economy in the EU's Eastern and Southern neighbourhood, and the "Four Common Spaces with Russia" which was particularly designed to address issues related to Russia.[23]

In addition, to further support the EU's objective in increasing its presence in the shared neighbourhood with Russia, the EU in 2008 launched another foreign policy instrument, namely the Eastern Partnership, which was intended to meet a purpose of integrating the EU more closely with its neighbours including Ukraine, Belarus, Moldova, Azerbaijan, Georgia, and Armenia.[24]

The above briefly illustrated the competitive relationship between the EU and Russia in order to augment the influence of each other in the post-Soviet space during the late 1990s and the early 2010s. Apparently, the EU had made enormous efforts to export its norms, values, and governance model mainly through a range of policy instruments; while Russia had attempted to mostly depend on the building of the Eurasian Customs Union to integrate Russia more closely with the former-Soviet republics.

Apart from the normative competition between the EU and Russia in the shared neighbourhood, security issue starting from the late 1990s had also become a growing concern for both sides, as a result of NATO expansion, as well as of the changing security situation in both the post-Soviet space and other regions of the globe.

In 2008, NATO at its Bucharest Summit announced the prospect of accepting Georgia and Ukraine as members. Given the significance of Ukraine to Russia in historical and strategic terms, all the security and economic issues related to Ukraine had gradually become a more crucial concern in the interactions between Russia and the west thereafter. At the early stage, Russia had tended to deal with Ukraine more from an economic dimension through the ECU/EEU.

2.2.2 The EU and the ECU/EEU over Issues Related to Ukraine

In the mid-1990s, Russia had already started to carry out a plan regarding forming an economic union/entity, through which, to tie Russia's economic interest with that of the newly independent states more closely; and a lot of efforts had been made by the relevant parties. However, till the late 1990s, no substantial progress had been made regarding the development of such an economic entity. After Russian President Putin came to power, Russia had begun to take concrete steps in progressing this matter. Following a series of efforts made by Russia and other partners including Belarus, Kazakhstan, Kyrgyzstan, and Tajikistan etc. throughout the late 1990s to the mid-2000s, the Eurasian Customs Union was established in October 2007. By the early 2010s, the ECU had achieved a big progress in standard setting and institutional building.[25]

Meanwhile, on the EU side, to move forward the implementation of the organization's Eastern Partnership policy, the EU and Ukraine from 2007 had begun to negotiate toward signing an Association Agreement.[26]

Based on a series of cost-benefit analysis and arguments made by some experts, it was very obvious that joining the ECU would put Ukraine in a more advantageous position than signing the AA with the EU by then.

First, from the political and systemic perspective, the ECU attached no political conditionality, while the AA attached a range of political conditions set by the EU.[27]

Second, the benefits for Ukraine by being a member of the ECU were even more appealing in economic and trade terms. Joining the ECU would help boom Ukraine's economy. The country's GDP would be expected to increase by $219 billion between 2011 and 2030. Besides that, the ECU would entitle Ukraine with even wider market access. In contrast, under the AA, the access of Ukrainian products to the EU market would be affected by the quotas set by the EU. Apart from that, according to the relevant cost-benefit analysis, the EU exports to Ukraine would likely surge by 10%, which would make Ukraine's GDP suffer up to 1.5% loss.[28]

Third, in accordance with Russia's planning, the ECU would be expected to serve as a vehicle in contributing to the progress of European integration from a broader dimension. In other words, the ECU could help facilitate the integration of its members with the EU, as President Putin pointed: "soon the Customs Union, and later the Eurasian Union will join the dialogue with the EU. As a result, apart from bringing direct economic benefits, accession to the Eurasian Union will also help countries integrate into Europe sooner and from a strategic position."[29]

The range of cost-benefit arguments made by some for joining the ECU in contrast to the protectionism of the EU, along with the tough negotiations in trade between the EU and Ukraine, had raised a lot of debates among the Ukrainian political and business elites. Some insisted to join the ECU; Some preferred to sign the AA with the EU; and some made the proposition of joining the ECU temporarily before being ready to sign the AA with the EU.[30] The ambiguous position of the Ukrainian side in trade negotiations with both Russia and the EU, as one observer argued, generally reflected "the continuing preference for a 'pick-and-mix' approach to economic integration that the country has demonstrated over the last 20 years [1991-2011] (an approach high on selectivity and low on commitment)."[31]

Overall, from the late 1990s to the early 2010s, economic issues and European integration had dominated the development trend of EU-Russia relations. Throughout this period, there was a growing competition between the EU and Russia in driving European integration in the shared neighbourhood.

Through that period of time, Russia generally wasn't opposed the idea of European integration. However, Russia's understanding to European integration was different from that of the EU. In line with the EU's design, European integration must have to set the European governance model and norms as a precondition for all its members and potential members. In contrast, Russia had appeared to promote a model of European integration from a broader spectrum by making the EU and the ECU inclusive with each other as well as without attaching any political conditionality.

2.2.3 U.S. and Russia during the Late 1990s and the Early 2010s: NATO Expansion and Colour Revolutions Driving the Rising Tension of U.S.-Russia Relations

In the late 1990s, a number of events such as the first wave of NATO expansion in 1999 by formally receiving Poland, Czech Republic, and Hungary as members, the Kosovo War, as well as other series of frictions occurred between the U.S. and Russia had driven the U.S.-Russia relations further down.

With the world stepping into the new century, the 9.11 terrorist attacks raised a possible hope for the two powers to improve their relations. President Putin became the first foreign leader to make a phone call to then U.S. President Bush.[32] The two countries declared to strengthen counter-terrorism cooperation, and to set a direction for a "new strategic partnership".[33] However, the spirit of sound cooperation didn't sustain long. Tension between the two sides once again emerged due to Russia's opposition to the U.S. invasion of Iraq in March 2003.[34]

The second wave of NATO expansion in 2004, alongside the pro-western "colour revolutions" supported by the U.S. in the post-Soviet space including the "rose revolution" in Georgia in 2003, the "orange revolution" in Ukraine in 2004, as well as the "colour revolution" in Kyrgyzstan in 2005 further escalated the tension between the U.S. and Russia.

Then four months after NATO's announcement of possibly offering membership to Georgia and Ukraine at the NATO Summit held in Bucharest in April 2008, Russia-Georgia conflict was erupted.

In 2011, more differences emerged between the U.S. and Russia, as a result of the "Arab Spring" colour revolutions involved by the U.S. in the Middle East, which led to a series of upheavals and mass anti-government protests across a number of Middle Eastern countries. As a consequence, the U.S.-led coalition dismantled the Muammar Qaddafi regime. Besides that, the U.S. had made attempt to change the Syrian Basharal Assad regime through supporting the anti-Assad government forces in Syria, which was also opposed by Russia.

Overall, from the late 1990s to the early 2010s, security issue had dominated the development of U.S.-Russia relations. Throughout this period, there had been an increasing tension between the U.S. and Russia, alongside the two countries competing for influence in the post-Soviet space. Apparently, three rounds of NATO expansion as well as the range of "colour revolutions" supported by the U.S. should be the main cause of the escalating tension between two countries.

2.2 Early 2010s - Present: Issues Related to Ukraine Gradually Taking the Central Stage

In the early 2010s, with regard to the matter of whether Ukraine should take steps toward joining the ECU or signing the AA with the EU, the Yanukovych government finally decided not to sign the agreement with the EU. Shortly thereafter, as supported by the western forces, a series of demonstrations opposing the government's failure to sign the AA took place in Ukraine, and ultimately led to the collapse of the Yanukovych government in early 2014.

Following that, Russia's intervention by taking control of Crimea, as well as the eruption of the conflict between Ukrainian government forces and anti-government forces in the Donbas region marked the full-scale breaking out of the first Ukraine crisis.

Since then, the issues related to Ukraine have come to the central stage in leading the development trend of Russia's relations with the west. The improper handling of the first Ukraine crisis by the concerned parties then partially led to the eruption of the second Ukraine crisis.

2.3.1 The EU and the U.S. on the First Ukraine Crisis

In response to the first crisis, the west used sanctions as a main tool in dealing with Russia. Along with the evolving situation in 2014, the EU and the U.S. had imposed three rounds of sanctions against Russia subsequently taken place in July, September, and December. The sanction measures taken by the EU and the U.S. were roughly the same, mainly targeting Russia's energy, defence, and financial industries, in addition to introducing visa bans and asset freezes on certain officials and individuals having close connection to Kremlin. The third round of sanctions imposed in December 2014 also introduced a ban on investment, trade, and tourism with Crimea.[35]

Though the U.S. and the EU adopted the similar sanction measures against Russia during and in the aftermath of the first Ukraine crisis, there was a difference between the two sides in their attitudes toward sanctioning Russia. Right after the breaking out of the crisis, the U.S. was more active in applying tough measures against Russia, as reflected by taking the initiative in imposing the first round of sanctions on 16 July 2014, and in the meantime by urging the EU to take the similar measures to deal with Russia. In contrast, on the EU side, given the closer linkage between the EU and Russia in various terms, the EU was reluctant to use sanctions against Russia.The EU side concerned that the sanction measures could affect the EU's long-term relations with Russia.[36]

Then, in the aftermath of the first Ukraine crisis, the EU and the U.S. also diverged regarding whether lifting the sanctions or not on Russia. The U.S. was affirmative in keeping the sanctions in place and had no inclination to lift the sanctions within a short-term.[37] In addition, the U.S. welcomed Ukraine's turn to the west and affirmed its support to the enhanced engagement between Ukraine and the EU, and between Ukraine and NATO.[38]

On the contrary, for the EU, given that the sanctions confronted the interests of the business communities of a number of EU members, there was a growing opposition within some EU countries to the sanctions. Certain countries were skeptical about the effectiveness of using sanctions in changing Russia's measures toward Ukraine. Some such as Italy, Greece, Cyprus, and Hungary complained about the impacts of the EU sanctions and Russia's counter-sanctions in response on their economies, so that pressed to ease the sanctions or to lift them all together. In addition, the French legislature passed a non-binding resolution urging the French government to support lifting the sanctions. Also, the German business community pressured the German government to lift the sanctions.[39]

Apparently, there had been a discrepancy between the U.S. and the EU in terms of their attitude toward using sanctions to deal with Russia during and in the aftermath of the first Ukraine Crisis. Some even worried that the sanctions might risk diverging the approaches taken by the EU and the U.S. toward Russia.[40]

To respond to the first Ukraine crisis, in addition to using sanctions to deal with Russia, both the EU and the U.S. had provided Ukraine with aids in various terms.

On the EU side, in March 2014, the European Commission offered an initial package of €11billion helping the reform process of then Ukrainian government. This package covered a €1.6 billion assistance loans to support the government macro-finances, and a €9 billion funded by the European Investment Bank and the European Bank for Reconstruction and Development to help improve Ukraine's infrastructure and transportation.[41] Apart from that, the EU offered to provide Ukraine with €1.5 billion in grant through the period between 2014 and 2020 to help the country's reforms.[42]

For the U.S. assistance to Ukraine, from the beginning of the crisis to around the late 2016, the U.S. had committed enormous support to Ukraine in financial, technical, and security terms.

The U.S. Agency for International Development (USAID) had been involved in helping deliver some of the U.S. economic and technical assistance to Ukraine. According to it, from the late 2013 to the end of U.S. then President Obama's term, the U.S. had provided Ukraine with more than $1.3 billion in economic assistance to help advance Ukraine's domestic reforms, strengthen Ukraine's governance capacity, and boost the country's economic growth etc.[43]

To further support the same purposes, apart from sending technical advisors to various levels of the Ukrainian government, the U.S. had offered three $1 billion loan guarantees to Ukraine.[44]

In terms of the U.S. security assistance to Ukraine, between 2014 and 2016, the U.S. had aided Ukraine with $600 million, which was mainly used in three areas: training Ukrainian soldiers, providing military equipment, and offering advice to Ukraine's defence reforms.[45]

2.3.2 The EU and the U.S. on the Second Ukraine Crisis

Upon the second Ukraine crisis, both the regional and international environment has changed quite a bit. Among a variety of factors which could affect the evolving trend of the second crisis, leaders of the main parties getting involved in managing this crisis would be the key factor in deciding how the second crisis can be developed and settled eventually.

As usual, following the breaking out of the crisis, both the EU and the U.S. have taken sanctions as a key measure in managing Russia. The sanction measures were further upgraded compared to those imposed over the first Ukraine crisis. The new measures, apart from targeting Russia's financial, defence, and energy sectors, also added the transportation sector on the list. As a result of the sanctions, Russia's state-owned enterprises, state-owned media agencies, and banks etc. have been affected. For instance, ten Russian banks have been banned from using the SWIFT system.[46]

Measures Taken by the EU in Dealing with the Second Ukraine Crisis

The repercussions generated by the sanctions and counter-sanctions would affect the European countries very seriously. Apart from the damages to the European economy, certain member states have been challenged by a lot of problems generated by the rising energy prices and food prices, as well as by the refugee crisis. To deal with these problems, alongside moving up sanction measures against Russia, the EU has taken a range of measures focusing on dealing with the crises related to energy and refugees. Besides that, the EU has managed to unlock more resources to fund Ukraine's armed forces.

As for the EU's assistance to the Ukrainian armed forces, from 28 February to mid-November 2022, the EU Council, under the European Peace Facility, had adopted six tranches of support packages to fund the Ukrainian armed forces, bringing this part of the EU's commitments to Ukraine to €3.1 billion. Besides this, on 15 November, the EU adopted two new measures including launching a special mission, namely the European Union Military Assistance Mission in Support of Ukraine (EUMAM Ukraine), as well as setting up an Assistant Measure to help further enhance the capacity building of the Ukrainian armed forces.[47]

With regard to addressing the refugee crisis, on 4 April, the European Council adopted a proposal on Cohesion's Action for Refugees in Europe (CARE), which would allow a quick release of funds to help the refugees. Under the CARE, the EU firstly allocated €17 billion; and then, to meet the same purpose and on the same day, the EU Council adopted another proposal to unlock up to €420 million under the home affairs funds. Apart from these, to further increase the flexibility in deploying the cohesion policy funds to address refugee-related issues, the European Council on 13 October adopted a set of legislative measures, one of which was related to allocating additional €3.5 billion to prefinance the relevant projects running from 2021 to 2027.[48]

In relation to managing the energy crisis faced by the EU in the near term, the European Council on 27 June adopted a regulation on filling gas storage levels by both the EU and its member states. In line with the regulation, every EU member state should make sure to fill at least 80% of its underground gas storage capacity before the winter of 2022/2023, and further 90% of the storage capacity before the following winter. Meanwhile, the EU should manage to meet 85% of the EU's underground gas storage capacity in 2022.[49] According to Gas Infrastructure Europe, by 21 November 2022, most of the EU members had met or surpassed the required levels of gas storage capacities; and in average the level of gas stored by the EU member states was above 94.8%.[50]

For the EU imports of gas and Liquefied Natural Gas (LNG) from the global market in 2022, according to the international media reports, as being affected by the ongoing Ukraine crisis, with the deducing EU imports of gas from Russia through pipe lines, Europe has increased its imports of LNG from both Russia and other countries. Between January and October, Europe's imports of LNG from the international market had been up by 70% in a year;[51] while Russia's share of the EU imports of LNG had surged by around 40% in a year.[52]

In addition, in order to prevent the surge of oil prices, on 3 December 2022, the European Council set a price cap on Russian oil at $60/barrel.[53] Shortly after that, on 4 December, in an international meeting held by the Organization of the Petroleum Exporting Countries (OPEC) and other key oil producing nations including Russia, the participating countries jointly stated to adhere to a previously agreed measure, which was set to cut oil production by 2 million barrels per day. This policy was adopted by OPEC and other major oil suppliers in October and came into effect in November.[54]

Apparently, Russia remains as an important energy supplier to Europe. Within a short-term, along with the on-going Ukraine crisis, as well as being affected by the evolving trend of the global market demands to energy, it would be hard for Europe to maintain a relatively stable energy price; and the EU would likely keep facing the similar pressure caused by the fluctuations of energy prices.

The U.S. Measures toward the Second Ukraine Crisis

In parallel with the range of actions taken by the EU in response to the second Ukraine crisis, the measures taken by the U.S. have mainly covered two aspects: sanctioning Russia and providing Ukraine with more assistance in budgetary and security terms.

For the sanctions against Russia, the U.S. and the EU have imposed the similar level of sanction measures. Yet, given that, in contrast to the EU, the U.S. has a low level of economic attachment with Russia, so Russia's counter-sanctions wouldn't likely cause a big impact on the U.S. in economic terms.

In terms of the U.S. assistance to Ukraine, from 4 March to 21 May, it had offered three core assistance packages related to Ukraine, which mainly consisted of three categories - humanitarian, economic, and security assistance.

On 4 March, the Biden Administration announced to add at least $10 billion in economic, humanitarian, and security assistance to Ukraine, of which, $4.8 billion would be committed to providing Ukraine with military equipment, as well as to supporting the deployment of the U.S. troops in Europe for better complementing the NATO efforts. Meanwhile, $5 billion out of the $10 billion assistance package would be related to helping boost the economy of both Ukraine and other regional allies, as well as to meeting humanitarian needs.[55]

Then on 16 March, the Biden government declared to add $800 million in security assistance to Ukraine, bringing the U.S. security assistance to Ukraine to a total of $2 billion since the Biden Administration took office. This part of the security assistance would be delivered in the form of military equipment.[56]

Further to the above, on 21 May, the U.S. President signed a bill to allocate another $40.1 billion in emergency funding for Ukraine, of which, $24.6 billion would be arranged for security assistance, and $15.5 billion would be for non-military operations.[57]

After then, the U.S. had added more assistance in various terms to Ukraine. From the outbreak of the second Ukraine crisis in February to the end of November, according to relevant reports, the U.S. Congress had passed a total of $66 billion in assistance to Ukraine; further to that amount, the White House has asked the Congress to approve additional $37.7 billion before 16 December to aid the Ukrainian government through the fiscal year of 2023.[58]

Generally, from the set of measures taken by both the U.S. and the EU in response to the second Ukraine crisis, we can see that the EU and the U.S. have different focus in dealing with the crisis. Due to the fact that the repercussions of the Ukraine crisis will impact on the U.S. and the EU in different ways, for the EU, apart from aiding Ukraine and sanctioning Russia, the EU in the meantime has spent a great deal of efforts on addressing the existing and potential implications of the evolving crisis to European countries in social, economic, humanitarian, and energy terms, as reflected by the series of measures adopted by the EU in handling the humanitarian and energy crisis.

While, for the U.S., besides providing Ukraine with humanitarian and economic assistance as well as imposing sanctions against Russia, the U.S. government has paid a lot of attention to the security assistance to Ukraine. There has been a dramatic surge in the U.S. security assistance related to the second Ukraine crisis, in contrast to the U.S. security support to Ukraine throughout the first Ukraine Crisis.

Then how has exactly the Ukraine crisis had, and will it continue to have an impact on the main parties involved in managing the crisis? The following part of this study will tend to address this issue. Given that the EU, Ukraine, and Russia will likely be more seriously affected by the crisis from the social and economic perspectives, it will only briefly analyse the impacts of the crisis on these three actors.

3. What Impacts Could the Ukraine Crisis Generate on Ukraine, Russia, and the EU?

3.1 Implications of the Ukraine Crisis to Ukraine

In the mid-2000s, as a result of a range of pro-western "colour revolutions" taking place in the post-Soviet space, issues related to Ukraine in the interactions between Russia and the west had started to become a bit more sensitive. In the following years after that, there had been numerous struggles occurring within Ukraine between the pro-western forces and the pro-Russia groups; and the series of internal and external struggles ultimately culminated in the first Ukraine crisis.

The first Ukraine crisis had dragged Ukraine into a recession. From Figure 1, we can see that both imports and exports of the country in goods had suffered a dramatic decrease during 2013-2015, with imports down from about $80 billion in 2013 to less than $40 billion in 2015, and with exports decreasing from over $60 billion to less than $40 billion throughout the same period. Besides that, the changes in exports and imports had almost been suspended during 2015-2016; then from 2016 to 2018, the country's exports and imports had secured a slow recovery, with imports increasing from around $40 billion in 2016 to less than $60 billion in 2018, and with exports rising from below $40 billion to less than $50 billion through the same duration.[59] Nonetheless, there was still a big gap from reaching back to the pre-crisis level in both exports and imports.

Figure 1: Ukraine: Imports and Exports of Goods, US$ millions, 2012-2018

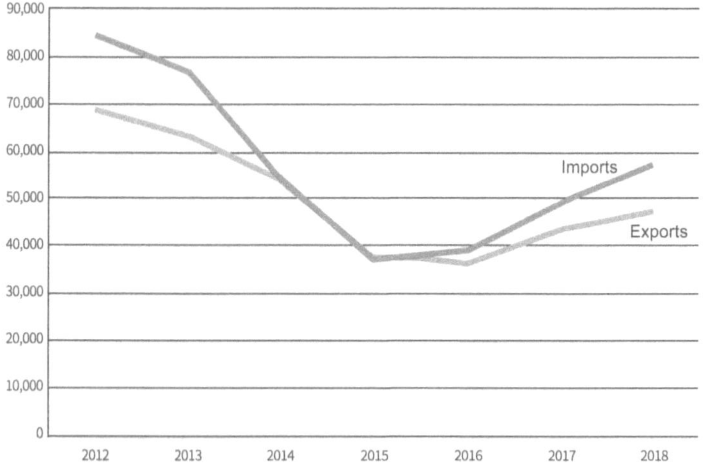

Figure 1 was cited from Marek Dabrowski, et al., July 2020.
Original Source: *World Bank World Integrated Trade Solution (WITS)*

From Figure 1, we can also see that even before the first crisis, Ukraine's exports and imports had already begun to drop. Apart from Ukraine's own reasons in economic performance, the country's deteriorating trade relations with Russia had contributed a significant part in leading to the dramatic decline of Ukraine's exports and imports.

Russia had long been a very important trade partner of Ukraine. Russia's sanctions on Ukraine in 2013 generated a 70% decrease of Ukraine's exports to Russia, constituting about an 18% drop in Ukraine's total exports the same year; following the eruption of the first Ukraine crisis, Ukraine's exports to Russia were further down by 50% in the year of 2014; then in January 2016, the Free Trade Agreement (FTA) between Russia and Ukraine was also suspended.[60] The suspension of the Russia-Ukraine FTA should have played a big role as well in the slow recovery of the Ukrainian exports and imports during 2016-2018.

Following the first crisis, Ukraine had tended to reorient the country's trade partners, yet building new commercial links would take time. Meanwhile, other factors such as the competitiveness of some of the Ukrainian products in the foreign markets including the EU market could also affect Ukraine's exports. It was estimated that losing a large part of the Russian market had led to a 6% drop in Ukraine's GDP.[61]

Before the Ukrainian government managed to make an improvement in the country's economic and trade performance, the COVID-19 pandemic has started to sweep through the world since the beginning of 2020. By 6 December 2022, the pandemic has taken about 110586 Ukrainian people's lives already.[62] The current ongoing Ukraine crisis somehow would continue to distract the government's efforts including allocating more resources in dealing with the pandemic. As a consequence of all these factors, Ukraine will certainly need a long period to recover, and further to build the country better.

When it relates to the repercussions of the second Ukraine crisis to Ukraine in economic terms, the International Monetary Fund (IMF) in April predicted that Ukraine would likely suffer a 35% loss in the country's GDP in 2022, while the World Bank in the same month estimated that Ukraine's economy in 2022 would drop by 45.1%.[63] As assessed by the Ukrainian side, by April the direct and indirect loss of the country had already surpassed $600 billion.[64]

In addition to the economic losses, Ukraine has also borne great human casualties. By the beginning of December 2022, according to relevant sources, more than 100,000 Ukrainian soldiers had died,[65] though the Ukrainian side hasn't officially released the number of combatant casualties. Apart from that, the war has also led to the casualties and displacements of a large number of civilian population. By 4 June - the date marking 100 days since the Russia-Ukraine war started on 24 February, according to the UNHCR, about 6.9 million Ukrainians had been forced by war to leave Ukraine, in addition to 8 million having been displaced within the country.[66]

Figure 2 gathered some information more recently released by *Statista* showing that, between 24 February and 29 November 2022, among the countries selected for having received a large number of

Ukrainian refugees, some 15838.85 thousand people had fled Ukraine for their neighbouring countries, with 8125.78 thousand of them having turned back to Ukraine over the same period.[67]

From Figure 2, we can also see that Poland is the country having ever received the largest number of civilians at around 7888.89 thousand, yet some 5806.16 thousand of whom had returned to Ukraine before 29 November.[68]

Figure 2: Number of Border Crossings between Ukraine and the Countries Selected, alongside the Russia-Ukraine War between 24 February and 29 November 2022 (in 1,000s)

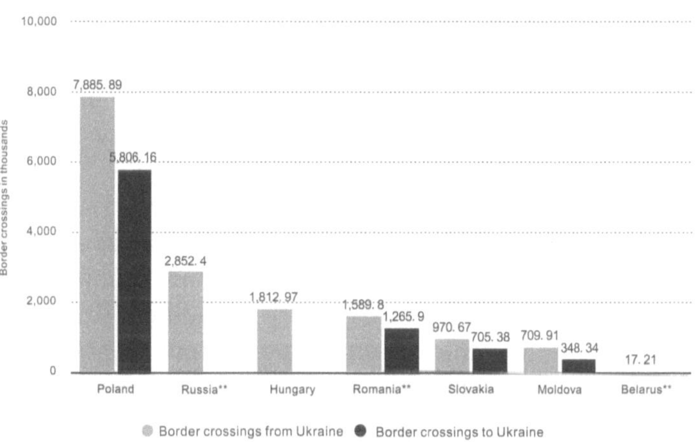

Source: *Statista,*
https://www.statista.com/statistics/1293403/cee-ukrainian-refugees-by-country/

3.2 Russia, Western Policies, and the Ukraine Crisis

To keep Russia as an influential power at both regional and global levels, apart from its military strength and nuclear capacity, three factors are considered very significant from the Russian perspective: domestic stability, economic prosperity, and a peaceful and stable security environment in Russia's surrounding areas.[69] Yet, since the 1990s, Russia has faced challenges in pursuing these three objectives. A significant part of the policies carried out by the U.S. and certain western countries since the late 1990s has sought to narrow Russia's strategic space in the post-Soviet region through NATO enlargement. This fact has threatened Russia's security interest from the Russian perspective. It ultimately culminated in the Russia-Georgia conflict, and then the first and second Ukraine crisis. Besides that, promoting the U.S.-led model of democracy within Russia as well as in the post-Soviet region through various means more or less has posed a challenge to Russia's interest in maintaining domestic stability. Further, the competition between Russia and the EU in the post-Soviet space somehow has affected the Russian government's efforts in smoothly proceeding the country's modernization process particularly in economic terms including optimizing Russia's economic structure over the years.

The policies developed by the U.S. and some western countries over the past years since the 1990s could have had an extended and deeper impact on Russia. From a certain sense, it may have affected Russia's choices in developing the country in a way that could better meet Russia's interest in some occasions.

In order to bring both internal and external matters back under control in the late 1990s and early 2000s, Russia has since then, under certain circumstances, tended to apply the country's comparative advantage in possessing rich energy resources to deal with the challenges posed by the U.S. and some western countries. Energy could be served as a foreign policy instrument by Russia in countering the sanctions imposed by the west.

In the meantime, the above measure could cause a problem for Russia itself, as from a certain degree, it would distract the government attention away from developing more comprehensively of other crucial sectors of the country. The mining sector of Russia nowadays still constitutes about 30% of the country's total federal tax revenue.[70] A large part of Russia's exports in goods are generated through trading in oil and gas. In 2021, exports of Russian oil and gas generated 49% of the country's total exports in goods, accounting for 14% of Russia's GDP.[71] In the same year, out of the €158 billion Russian exports in goods to the EU, which was by then Russia's largest trade partner, €98.9 billion - 62% of the total - were contributed by mineral fuels.[72]

With regard to the impact of the first Ukraine crisis on Russia, it was estimated that, as a result of the western sanctions and also the reciprocal sanctions of Russia against the west over the first Ukraine crisis had led to a loss of 6% in Russia's GDP between 2014 and 2018.[73]

The second Ukraine crisis is still ongoing. According to World Bank's forecast in earlier 2022, Russia's economy will likely shrink by 11.2% in 2022.[74]

Other various problems caused by the sanctions and counter-sanctions between the west and Russia have appeared as well. For example, like many other countries, Russia has also faced pressure in dealing with the inflation problem. Figure 3 showed that Russia's inflation rate, in contrast to the same month of 2021, had a dramatic surge from 9.2% in February to 17.8% in April 2022, thereafter started to steadily decline, and was down to 12.7% by October 2022 under certain measures taken by the government apparently.[75]

Given that the major factors that have contributed to the rising inflation including the pandemic, and the ongoing Russia-Ukraine conflict, as well as a series of other existing and potential reasons would continue to play a role in affecting inflation in the coming 2023, a large number of countries including Russia would still need to devote some energy in managing this issue.

Figure 3: Russia: Inflation rate from September 2021 to October 2022 (compared to the same month of the previous year)

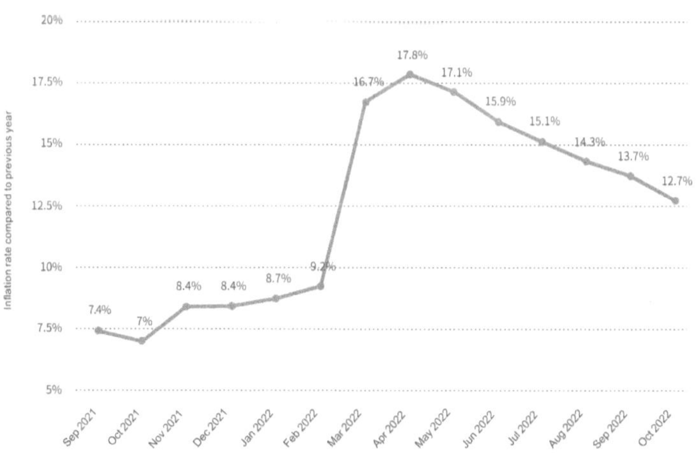

Source: *Statista,*
https://www.statista.com/statistics/276323/monthly-inflation-rate-in-russia/

Generally, sanctions and counter-sanctions would generate vulnerabilities for both Russia and its western counterparts in various ways. Since the outbreak of the second Ukraine crisis, both Russia and the west have managed to frozen certain amount of each other's assets. For the Russian side, so far more than $330 billion Russian assets have been frozen by the west.[76] Besides that, another challenging issue as a consequence of the sanctions that Russia will have to deal with could be related to the shrinking of the European investments flowing into Russia. The EU is a very important investor in Russia, and was the largest one in 2019; and by that year, the EU Foreign Direct Investment outward stock in Russia reached €311.4 billion.[77] As being affected by the sanctions, certain European business investors' choices in investing in Russia would be constrained; and in that regard, Russia could face a challenge of deploying more European capital to develop the country's economy in the coming years, as far as the relevant sanctions are implemented and sustained.

3.3 The Cost of the EU as A result of the Ukraine Crisis

Following the eruption of the Russia-Ukraine conflict, the EU till early December 2022 has imposed nine rounds of sanction measures against Russia. Based on careful calculation, some of the EU's sanctions, which wouldn't likely severely damage the EU's interests, have been implemented.

Before the second Ukraine crisis, Russia was the EU's number one energy supplier, and 66% of the EU oil and gas were provided by Russia.[78] According to the pre-crisis data, generally there was a big variation in the degree of EU member states' dependency on Russian oil and gas. The major European powers like Germany and Italy had a greater dependency on Russian oil and gas than some others such as Finland and the Baltic states.[79] For instance, for Italy, gas accounted for about 40% of the country's energy mix; for Germany, it constituted more than 25% of Germany's total energy mix; over 60% of German gas and 45% of Italy's were supplied by Russia in 2020.[80] These numbers could tell that the European members like Italy and Germany would be more vulnerable in facing Russia's counter-measures.

Russia's total fossil energy exports to the EU in 2021 amounted to more than €110 billion, constituting about 0.7% in average of European GDP.[81] Given that the EU members had various degrees of dependency on Russian energy, for some states, the shares of their imported Russian energy corresponded to around 2% of their countries' GDP.[82]

Overall, due to the importance of Russian energy to the EU countries, since the crisis started, the EU has carefully managed its measures related to Russian energy. So far the EU hasn't issued any sanctions on Russian gas. Before securing enough security in energy, the EU will not be prepared to do so.

Following the outbreak of the Ukraine crisis, as being influenced by the sanctions and counter-sanctions between Russia and the EU as well as by the explosion of a certain part of the natural gas pipelines, the amount of Russian natural gas flowing to Europe through pipelines has been dwindled. To offset the repercussions led by the shrinking Russian gas volumes, the EU countries have significantly increased their imports of LNG from other countries including Russia between February and October 2022.

In the coming years, as far as the EU issues or tightens any measures related to Russian oil and gas, potentially, the EU members would likely bear a higher cost or face more uncertainties, as the shortage of energy would drive the energy prices to surge; and then the civilian use of energy as well as the regular economic development of a number of EU member states would be affected by the rising energy prices.

At the beginning of December, the EU imposed a price cap on Russian oil of $60 per barrel. The issue of how likely the cap can be kept in the coming months would much depend on the development trend of the following crucial matters at least - the overall global economic situation,measures taken by the U.S. in relation to oil in the coming 2023, measures of the OPEC plus, and the evolving situation of the Russia-Ukraine conflict etc.

From the beginning of 2020 to 5 December 2022, as shown in Figure 4, the oil price in average had exhibited a rising trend generally. In early 2020, as being influenced by the initial shock of the COVID-19 pandemic, there was a sharp decrease of global demands in oil, and the oil price was then down to its lowest level on 20 April 2020 in a three-year period, at $25.57 with Brent oil, $14.19 with OPEC Basket, and $-37.63 with WTI. After then, the average oil price had started to increase.[83]

Figure 4 also indicated that, the outbreak of the Ukraine crisis resulted in a quick surge of oil prices in a very short period of time from around $100.00 on 28 February, to more than $120.00 on 7 March.

From then on till early December 2022, the prices had started to fluctuate with an incrementally declining trend.[84] Apart from other series of reasons such as the general global economic recession, the measures taken by the U.S. are assumed to have played an important part in affecting the evolving trend of the oil prices between March and December 2022.

Figure 4: Closing Price of Brent, OPEC Basket, and WTI Crude Oil at the Beginning of Each Week from 2 March 2020 to 28 December 2022 (in U.S. dollars per barrel)

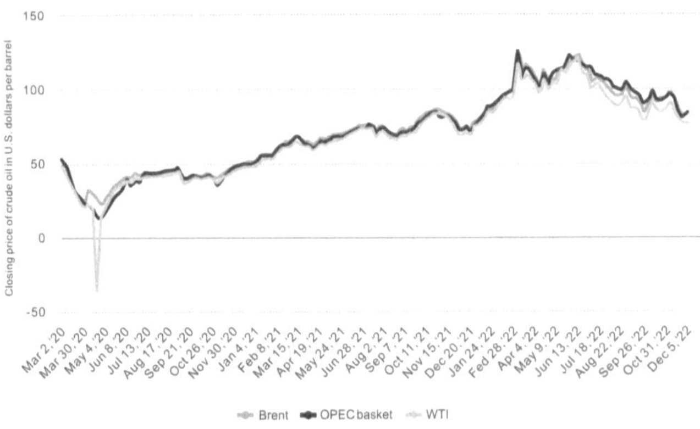

Source: *Statista*
https://www.statista.com/statistics/326017/weekly-crude-oil-prices/

On 1 March 2022, the U.S. government announced that the United States and other member countries of the International Energy Agency (IEA) would commit to collectively release 60 million barrels of oil from their national strategic oil reserves to counter the disruption of global energy supply led by the Ukraine crisis.[85] Then at the end of March, the U.S. government issued a measure to release 1 million barrels of oil per day from the U.S. strategic reserve for six months.[86] Between 4 March and 14 October, the U.S. had released a total of 172.4 million barrels. Further, on 19 October 2022, the U.S. government added 15 million barrels of oil to be released from the strategic reserve in the following month.[87]

In addition to the measures taken by the U.S. government, the U.S.

oil producing companies, as part of the reactive measures to the Ukraine crisis, have increased their oil production by 1 million barrels per day in 2022, and will further add 700, 000 barrels per day in 2023.[88]

The above range of measures were set to stabilize global oil prices, as well as to shrink the amount of Russian oil revenue for funding Russia's war in Ukraine.

From the U.S. perspective, the U.S. has an intention to push the oil prices further down, because apart from serving the purpose of stabilizing the global energy market and of preventing Russia from receiving more oil revenue at the current moment, as the media revealed, the U.S. Energy Department will aim to use the revenue obtained from the large scale of oil release to replenish the U.S. strategic reserve in the future, should the oil prices be pressed to a sufficiently low level.[89]

Anyway, alongside the U.S. government ordering to release the country's strategic oil reserve, the OPEC countries plus a number of major oil producing states agreed a policy in October to constrain oil supply by 2 million barrels per day. This measure just came into effect in November 2022, and was expected to be carried out till the end of 2023.

Overall, given the above complicated situation, for the time being, it is still early to say how likely the U.S. policies, the OPEC Plus measures, the global economic situation, and the Ukraine crisis could continue to impact on the oil prices in the coming year. The issue of whether and how the $60 cap on Russian oil set by the EU could work would be subject to the mixed interactions of these factors.

With regard to the changes of gas prices, Figure 5 showed that, between January 2020 and September 2022, the average gas price had depicted a growing trend with big fluctuations taking place in 2022.[90]

From Figure 5, we can also see that there was a sharp increase in the gas price index between May 2022 and August 2022 in particular. Then, it started to drop dramatically, yet the gas prices in September and October 2022 were still a lot higher than the average price in 2020 and 2021 respectively.[91]

It is assumed that European countries' growing demands in gas for filling the required levels of underground gas storage capacities before the winter of 2022 had significantly contributed to the dramatic surge of gas prices from May to August in 2022.

Figure 5: Monthly Natural Gas Price Index Worldwide from January 2020 to October 2022

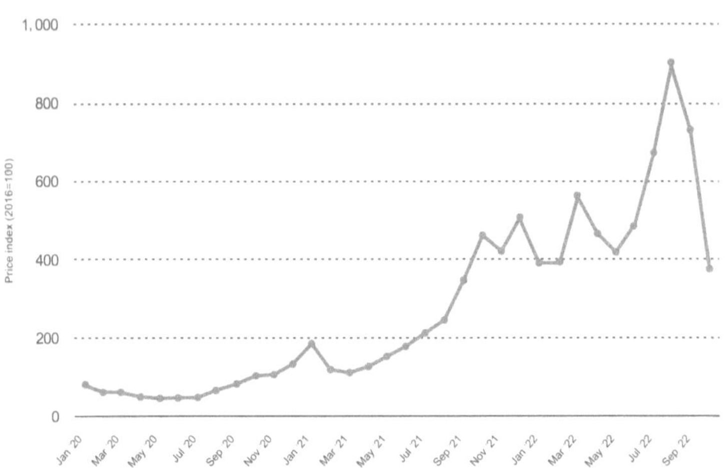

Source: *Statista*
https://www.statista.com/statistics/1302994/monthly-natural-gas-price-index-worldwide/

With the shrinking Russian gas volumes to Europe, the EU countries' rising demands in LNG from other markets made the U.S. become the largest LNG supplier to the EU, constituting around 42% of the EU's total LNG imports between January and October 2022.[92] In 2023, the U.S. would likely continue to be a major LNG supplier to Europe. Under this circumstance, in the coming year, Russia would divert a significant part of its gas either in the form of LNG or through pipelines to other markets as well, especially, Asia.

Then what would be the impacts on some European countries by shifting their primary gas supplier from Russia to the U.S.?

Economically, Europe will prepare to continue to face unstable gas prices, and to bear more costs in average generally in a foreseeable term. Gas prices in other regions would likely be affected by the fluctuations in demands and supplies of gas in Europe as well. The energy security issue would possibly further escalate the tension between Russia and some EU members. In that regard, the development of the situation in Europe would confront Europe's long-term interest in seeking a enduring peace in Europe.

In addition, as being influenced by the repercussions of the Ukraine crisis, the energy security issue would also affect the pace of European countries' efforts in seeking a clean and low carbon development.

According to the U.S. Energy Information Administration, the U.S. was the number one oil producer in 2021, with an output of 18.98 million barrels daily, while Saudi Arabia and Russia were on the second and third place behind the U.S., with an output of 10.83 million and of 10.77 million respectively per day.[93] The U.S. oil output in 2022 has been further expanded, as the U.S. companies have increased oil production by 1 million barrels per day in response to the Ukraine crisis. Besides the oil production, some analysts predicted that the U.S. LNG exports will expect to reach 151.59 billion cubic feet per day, in contrast to 143.23 billion cubic feet daily in 2022, and 116.84 billion cubic feet per day in 2021.[94]

These numbers can tell that, as far as there is a demand, more U.S. fossil fuels will be ready to go to other regions including Europe in the coming 2023. Increasing outputs of fossil fuels would not be conducive to the global efforts in seeking green development, and would undermine the climate actions already taken by a number countries, especially, European states, which have long been advocating for low carbon growth.

After all, solely shifting a significant part of energy dependence from Russia to the U.S. in order to meet a short-term interest would not be able to fundamentally solve the energy security issue faced by Europe from a long-term perspective. Even worse, it may potentially create a number of new problems for both Europe and the globe. Therefore, for the interests of all sides, it would be better for major European powers to adopt a more peaceful and workable approach toward settling down the Ukraine crisis as well as for addressing their current contentious relations with Russia.

In addition to the energy crisis, a refugee crisis has occurred already. Alongside the ongoing Ukraine crisis, the EU has already taken a range of measures including unlocking more funding sources to address the refugee issue. Nevertheless, it may take some time for the repercussions of the refugee crisis to appear; and the extended consequences of the refugee issue could have a long-term impact on the societies of some European states.

Overall, the potentially extended repercussions of the energy crisis and of the refugee crisis as well as of other possible conundrums generated by the Ukraine crisis could risk getting Europe into a situation, in which, apart from bearing the social and economic costs, major European powers would also be forced by a growing difficult situation to slow down the process in their joint efforts to pursue collective strategic autonomy, and to make the EU one of the most important and influential entities or poles in a multi-polar global system.

Then what will be the next related to the Ukraine crisis? Whether are there any possible means to help get the parties concerned out of the current crisis, and more crucially, to be able to serve a long-term interest of all relevant parties based on taking into consideration their main concerns?

4. Possible Way out for the Ukraine Crisis & the Prospect of A New European Order and beyond

4.1 The Primary Concern of and Key Problems of Ukraine

Following the dissolution of the former Soviet Union, like other former Soviet republics, Ukraine entered a transformation period. Yet the path for transforming Ukraine into a stable and prosperous country over the past decades has proved to be very challenging.

In the aftermath of the first Ukraine crisis, the Ukrainian people elected a pro-western Poroshenko government. Nevertheless they didn't seem to trust the Poroshenko government's capacity in addressing the country's corruption as well as in implementing the relevant reform programmes, as reflected by the fact that, by then, both the judicial and executive systems of Ukraine received a low supporting rate of the Ukrainian people. The former U.S. assistant Secretary of State Nuland, in the process of carrying out the reforms in Ukraine, ever indicated in October 2015 that "only 5% of the Ukrainian population completely trusted the judiciary."[95] Meanwhile, in November 2015, in a public survey conducted by the Rating Group of Ukraine for the International Republican Institute, then President Poroshenko and then Prime Minister Yatsenyuk respectively obtained a 27% and a 12% positive rate among those who participated.[96]

Anyway, in order to make Ukraine a peaceful, stable, and prosperous country, Ukraine through the past years has made numerous external and internal struggles. In the meantime, to support Ukraine's reform process as well as the country's turn to the west, the U.S. and a number of western partners have been regularly aiding Ukraine via various forms, especially, since the first Ukraine crisis, the U.S. and some western countries have further expanded the scope of assistance to Ukraine, as having already outlined in the previous part of this study.

However, after all these years of reforms as well as under the enormous amount of aid offered by the west to Ukraine, issues related to addressing corruption and improving governance capacity still prove to be the critical factors in undermining the country's efforts in achieving stability and prosperity of the country. Ukraine apparently is still struggling to find the right means to deal with these challenges.

Then, what have mainly affected the government's reform process? There might be numerous reasons behind this question, one of which should be related to independent decision-making of the government in the reform process. Ukraine's reform process has been greatly influenced by the west. The western economic and technical assistance to support Ukraine's reforms usually attached a number of conditions. The implementation of the relevant aid projects was also under the guidance of the west. Ukraine didn't have the full-right in determining how the western funding can be utilized, and how the relevant reform programmes can be implemented. These meant that Ukraine's reforms have to be carried out mostly in accordance with the standards, index, or numbers set by the western governments or institutions.

Under these circumstances, the efficiency in deploying the internal and external sources to carry out reforms could be undermined. The inefficient use of western funding, instead of fighting corruption, could feed corruption. Without the full-right of self-determination, improving governance capacity should become very challenging.

Another serious risk as driven by the above scenario could be that in order to secure enough funding to carry out the reforms, the Ukrainian institutions, within a particular period of time, may strive hard to meet the conditions set by the western governments or institutions; then once the funding is delivered to Ukraine, or the internal and external situation of Ukraine is changed, the positive outcomes achieved previously might risk being reversed or deduced. In this case, relevant reforms could be taken as a matter of expediency. As a consequence, real and substantial reforms cannot be achieved. These are not conducive to the real improvement of governance capacity after all.

Ukraine has actually long been facing the very much similar problems in the reform process as other former Soviet republics had met in the 1990s. Others have managed to overcome a large part of the same challenges over the past decades. For Ukraine, in the coming years, apart from maintaining a strong political will, trying to attain the full-right of self-determination, establishing an accountable governance system, cultivating a range of accountable institutions to guarantee the implementation of the core reforms, as well as forming a sound supervision system should be of great significance in deciding whether the Ukrainian government will be able to attain great success in proceeding reforms.

Furthermore, another challenging factor that has constrained the Ukrainian government's efforts in promoting reforms and achieving greater economic progress of the country is that the decision-makers in some occasions allowed the "either white or black" logic, rather than the real interest of the country, to influence key policy-making.

For instance, with regard to the debate years ago that whether Ukraine should join the Eurasian Economic Union led by Russia, or sign an Association Agreement (AA) with the EU, as being affected by the "either white or black" logic, this matter finally turned out that, from the Ukrainian perspective, being part of the EEU meant an opposition to the EU's AA, or signing the AA meant opposing the EEU.

For the interest of the country as well as of the Ukrainian people, signing the AA with the EU and joining the EEU shouldn't be confrontational. Apparently, the Ukrainian government's decision over this matter so far hasn't been able to serve the country's interest well.

The AA between Ukraine and the EU was singed in 2014, and officially came into force in September 2017. More than five years on, Ukraine didn't appear to have benefited from the AA very significantly, in particular, concerning the issue of trade with the EU members. Partly as a result of certain restrictive measures in trade set by the EU, Ukraine has had a trade deficit with the EU in both goods and services over the years.

The agriculture sector should be a comparative advantage of

Ukraine, yet, the access of the country's agriculture products to the EU market has been restricted. In contrast, being a member of the EEU, Ukraine would have been authorized a wider access to the markets of the EEU members.

In response to the ongoing second Ukraine crisis, as part of the EU's assistance packages to Ukraine, the organization has set a duty-free measure on all Ukrainian products exporting to the EU countries for one year. Given the current domestic situation in Ukraine, at what level this assistance measure of the EU could help improve Ukraine's trade in 2022 remains to be seen. Generally, to properly manage the trade relations between the EU and Ukraine, and to meet the interests of both sides in a more balanced manner, they will still need to take a lot of steps in the years to come.

After all, in the years ahead, struggling to fix the number of problems encountered by the country through the past years of reform process since the 1990s by exercising a more effective, accountable, and inclusive governance should be the key in eventually helping the government reach the goal of making Ukraine a peaceful, stable, and wealthy country.

4.2 How Could the EU and Russia Jointly Develop An Improved Interactive Approach?

In the early years after the disintegration of the former Soviet Union, the EU and Russia had ever held high expectations to each other - the EU had anticipated to transform Russia in line with the EU-designed model, and eventually to make Russian be part of the European order driven by the EU; in the meantime, Russia had also expected to adopt a different approach in order to regain its national strength, particularly, in economic terms, even though from the very beginning of the 1990s, Russia had already stated not to compromise Russia's sovereignty to develop a relationship with the EU.

In the later stage of the 1990s, the transformation process hadn't gone the way as both Russia and the EU expected. Discrepancies between the two sides had emerged concerning the integrated relationship between Russia and the EU as well as the process in driving European integration. Thereafter, the EU-Russia relationship had become more competitive. Further, starting from the late 1990s, the EU had developed a series of policy instruments to manage its relationship and cooperation with Russia.

Over the past three decades, the development of Russia-EU relations hasn't always gone smoothly in general terms, with tensions being raised from occasion to occasion. Nevertheless, the two sides in the meantime have also managed to develop a close collaboration from the economic, trade, tourism, research, and education dimensions. In terms of Russia-EU economic and trade relations, according to the data collected before the outbreak of the second Ukraine crisis, the EU was Russia's largest trading partner, Russia was the EU's fifth largest one, and Russia was also the EU's number one energy supplier.[97] In relation to short-term education exchanges, among the 130 countries joining in the EU's Erasmus+ programme, Russia had the largest number of participants.[98] Regarding travel and tourism, in 2019 the number of Schengen visas issued to Russian citizens surpassed 4 million, listing on the top, and accounting for 27% of total Schengen visas issued across the globe.[99]

In response to the the second Ukraine crisis, the EU has tightened certain measures on issuing visas to Russian citizens. The tourism sectors of Russia and some European countries would have been influenced, along with the ongoing crisis. Besides this, the sanctions and counter-sanctions have already seriously damaged the economic and trade relations as well as exchanges in other variety of areas between Russia and the EU.

Under the current contentious situation, how the EU and Russia could jointly work out an approach to settle down the ongoing Ukraine crisis could not only have a significant impact on the interests of the EU and Russia, but also on the possible shaping of a new European order in the future, and even of a Eurasian order from a broader perspective.

Over the past years, Russia has long been setting a strategic objective of maintaining Russia's regional and international influence, and of making Russia be recognized as one of the major poles in a multi-polar global system; the EU has also been proved to have an ambition of expanding its influence through exporting the EU standards and model through the same period.

For the interest of the European continent, there is a need for the EU, Russia, and other major European powers to manage to peacefully coexist and further to jointly shape a new European order. One of the most serious challenges faced by the EU is that it appears to lack a confident collective leadership as well as a clear direction about the organization's future. There is a division within the EU regarding this matter - some would prefer to tie the EU's interests with that of the U.S.-led transatlantic design; some would seek to consolidate the strategic autonomous status of Europe, and some could have taken into account other possible options such as engaging the EU's future more closely with a broader Eurasian arrangement etc.

Under the current circumstances, addressing the Ukraine crisis can be a test for the EU, Russia, and other major European powers. The EU and Russia have reached a very critical point, upon which, both sides are in need to explore a new or an improved approach to deal with each other. It should be different from the one having been deployed by the major powers throughout the Cold War period. That means, instead of continuing to follow the traditional path in repeating the game of great power competition and in attaching great significance to the pursuit of sphere of influence, it is in need for the EU and Russia to jointly develop a more inclusive approach, which is expected to be conducive to the consolidation of the EU's strategic autonomy as well as to the future interests of the whole European continent.

To meet the above purpose, the approach developed by ASEAN can be well-shared with the EU. Even though the EU over the past years has made a great progress in promoting European integration, a lot of problems alongside this process have also emerged. In this regard, some of the experiences accumulated by ASEAN, in particular, in relation to ASEAN's management of its relations with the major powers, should be applicable to the EU as well.

ASEAN generally has been successful in managing its foreign relations with the major powers in Asia and in other continents, as well as in keeping the status of the ASEAN Centrality and strategic autonomy in the process of engaging with various partners. ASEAN has also made some fruitful achievements in promoting regional economic integration through forging a "ASEAN Plus" model together with other powers in Asia.

In line with the "ASEAN Plus" model, the ten ASEAN nations and China constituted a "ASEAN Plus One" cooperation mechanism; then the ASEAN together with China, Japan, and South Korea forged a "ASEAN Plus Three" mechanism; further the Regional Comprehensive Economic Partnership (RCEP) agreement came into force by including the ASEAN nations and China, Japan, South Korea, Australia, and New Zealand as its members.

The "ASEAN Plus" model can be explicitly characterized as "be with the ASEAN", rather than, "be part of the ASEAN". This model has so far dramatically paved the way for ASEAN and its partners to shape each other's interests.

For a more certain future of the European continent, for peacefully promoting European integration in the years ahead, and further for shaping a new European order and beyond, the EU, Russia, and other major European powers will need to take into account jointly exploring a more inclusive approach to interact with each other, which can also be mapped as a model of "be with the EU", rather than "be part of the EU".

4.3 The Relevance of the Settlement of the Ukraine Crisis to the United States, Russia, and Europe and beyond

Since the end of WWII, the U.S. policy toward Europe hasn't fundamentally changed. It has mainly centred on two aspects: keeping consolidating and expanding the U.S. influence in Europe; and competing with the former Soviet Union for strategic dominance before 1991, and then seeking to narrow Russia's strategic space in the post-Soviet region after 1991.

Over the past decades, the U.S. has manged to deal with Russia mostly from the strategic, economic, and security dimensions. NATO, among a wide variety of networks and organizations, has played a very crucial part not only from the security sense in the U.S. favour, but also in relation to the promotion of U.S. democratic values in the wider post-Soviet space. In economic terms, the U.S. has relied on its dominant position in a number of global institutions/organizations such as the IMF, WTO, and WB to project the U.S. influence, and to bind the U.S. interests with those of Europe. In the meantime, in order to complicate Russia's strategic economic interests, the U.S. has attempted to dissuade European countries from depending on Russian energy.

Currently against the backdrop that the U.S. has shifted a big part of its strategic priorities to Asia and is planning to deepen the implementation of its Indo-Pacific strategy, the outcomes the U.S. has secured so far through implementing its Cold War policy in Europe over the past decades are assumed to carry a critical symbolic meaning for the U.S., as from the U.S. perspective, they would be conducive to the U.S.'s efforts in further framing and implementing its Indo-Pacific strategy in the coming steps.

As the U.S. claimed in a report on its Indo-Pacific strategy, instead of seeking to change China, the U.S. aims to alter the strategic environment in which China operates. Starting from the mid-1990s, the U.S. exactly has been making a great deal of attempts to alter the strategic space in which Russia has operated through carrying out a range of policy measures including enlarging NATO, supporting the former eastern bloc states' turn to the west, as well as launching "colour revolutions" in the post-Soviet space and so on.

Anyway, the above seemingly positive outcomes from the U.S. perspective just depicted one side of the picture. On the other side of it, the U.S. policy measures toward Europe since the end of WWII have also constituted serious problems from the economic, social, security, and strategic perspectives.

With regard to the economic consequences of the U.S. measures more recently in handling the Ukraine crisis, the U.S. intention to weaken Russia has in reality weakened its European allies also, and has put Europe in a more fragile situation. Sanctioning Russia also means sanctioning the EU member states. The EU countries would likely bear more severe consequences from a long-term perspective; and the countries in other regions could be affected as well under certain circumstances, as already assessed in great details in the previous part of this research.

For serving a long-term strategic economic interest of the U.S., after WWII, the country had led to constitute a series of critical global institutions/organizations including the IMF, the WB, and the WTO etc., through which, the U.S. anticipated to bind the U.S. interests with those of its western allies. Through the past years, even though the U.S. has managed to sustain its dominance in these global institutions, a number of issues have also been emerged within these organizations, in particular, with regard to the aspect of how to move forward the reform process of these institutions in order to make them more adaptable to the new situation. Frictions have been raised between the U.S. and Europe concerning the matter of various reforms from occasion to occasion. The U.S. policy shift to Asia for seeking other opportunities since the beginning of the 2010s partly has reflected the U.S. inability to fix some of the serious challenges in other parts of the world including Europe.

Moreover, the series of attempts made by the U.S. to narrow Russia's strategic space in Europe and to prevent Russia and some

European states from getting closer through various means including NATO enlargement since the 1990s have from a certain sense pushed Russia to seek opportunities beyond the European region. Since the beginning of the new century, Russia has gradually engaged more closely with various partners including the emerging economies based in other regions.

From the security dimension, unlike the U.S. wanted, the enlargement of NATO hasn't brought peace and stability to Europe. The NATO expansion has led to a more fragile security situation in Europe. Currently, as led by the ongoing Ukraine crisis, there are people either dying or being displaced everyday, and a number of European countries and residents have been challenged by various crises from time to time and from occasion to occasion. Unfortunately, there is still no clear sign when the Ukraine crisis can be put to an end.

Under the above circumstances, it would be inappropriate to take NATO expansion as a positive strategic outcome of the United States; and also it wouldn't be proper to make such an outcome serve as a symbolic meaning of the U.S. strength or power to further pave the way for the U.S. implementation of its Indo-Pacific strategy in the years ahead.

Anyway, with regard to the settlement of the Ukraine crisis, at least three type of scenarios might occur. The first one would be that if the major European powers manage to take the main position in helping settle down the Ukraine crisis, a common understanding between Ukraine and Russia and between Russia and the EU would be reached; and then the EU and Russia in that respect would more likely be able to find a better way to deal with each other. This outcome would serve well of the EU's interest in raising the organization's status at both regional and international levels. More crucially, for the EU, it would be a very significant initial step toward shaping a new European order.

The second scenario could be that Russia and Ukraine are able to take control of this matter by themselves through diplomatic consultation step by step. This way of settling down the crisis can help generate a lot more certainties for future relations of the two countries. Settling down the current crisis by themselves would also create a good pre-condition for the two sides to recover their economic and trade relations as well as to widen their cooperation in other range of areas.

In relation to addressing the Ukraine crisis, a few months before the four regions of Ukraine, consisting of Lugansk, Donetsk, Zaporozhye, and Kherson, voted to re-join the Russian Federation in late September, the U.S. former Secretary of State Henry Kissinger in his speech in May 2022 at the World Economic Forum advised that "ideally, the dividing line should return to the former status quo,"[100] which was understood that, for ending the war, Russia and Ukraine should manage to return to their positions before Russia began to carry out its special military operation on 24 February.

Then, the referendums held in the above four regions added more complication for the bilateral settlement of the Ukraine crisis. According to the media reports, the U.S. officials ever pressed Ukraine to start negotiating with Russia. Yet the Ukrainian side was not ready for that. Then, on 16 December, in an interview at the Carnegie Endowment Think Tank, the U.S. National Security Advisor Jake Sullivan claimed that the moment for negotiation is "not right now", and that "it's our job to continue to sustain our military support to Ukraine, so they are in the best possible position on the battlefield, so that if and when the diplomacy is ripe, they will be in the best possible position at the negotiating table."[101]

Apparently, the current situation is that Ukraine is not prepared for negotiation yet, as far as its demands from Russia cannot be properly met. Under this condition, Ukraine would keep asking for assistance from the U.S., and in the meantime, the U.S., under the current U.S. Administration, would be ready to sustain its military support to Ukraine as long as it can. While for the Russian side, Russia is not ready to compromise the country's position as well. Hence, the Ukraine crisis is being trapped in a stalemate now.

Under such circumstances, more likely we would see a third scenario to happen. It means that the Russia-Ukraine conflict could be turned into a long-lasting war; and along with the time moving, sporadic fighting between Russia and Ukraine would become a primary phenomenon, with heavy fighting and strikes to take place only upon certain occasions. This scenario also means that, within a short-term, there will likely be no consensus reached between Russia and Ukraine, and the chaotic situation in Ukraine will remain for a long time to come, unless there could be a leadership change in the coming years either in the U.S., or in Ukraine, or in Russia, which might create a possibility for ending the Russia-Ukraine war at an earlier date.

Anyway, ultimately a strong, independent, and peaceful Europe in the long future, apart from its power in economic and financial terms, will have to meet at least three conditions. First, Russia and the EU will need to peacefully coexist and to jointly facilitate each other's interests, rather than attempt to beat each other. Second, an improvement of collective leadership among the major European powers will be essential. Third, from a long-term perspective, there is a need for European countries to take into account developing their own security system and building their own platform for political and security dialogue (a platform like the ASEAN Regional Forum), which should be conducive to the forging of a more united Europe. The NATO members should feel free to join Europe's own security system, or to continue to stay as NATO members.

As far as the above conditions can be met, Europe, as a more united entity, in a long-term future will have more freedom to choose which partners to engage with across the world. If these conditions cannot be reached in the future, we may likely see a more fragmented Europe, which means that, economically a number of individual European states might be growing stronger, yet politically the whole Europe will have no collective leadership.

If a more united Europe cannot be attained in the future, besides the above, there could be another case to occur, which is that the same "transatlantic story" will last for some time. It means that the nature of the transatlantic relations will have no big change, and that what have been happening in Europe since the end of WWII will likely repeat. Generally, this scenario hasn't been in the overall interest of Europe.

Then, even under the above conditions, there might still be a possibility for a Quasi-multi-polar system to be shaped in the future. It means that the U.S. will still be the most powerful country, yet from a relative and comparative perspective, the U.S. global influence in both substantial and symbolic terms will keep declining. In the meantime, the power of other major powers and entities such as India, Japan, ASEAN, and the EU etc. will be growing in contrast to their strength in the previous years.

Together with the U.S., other main actors such as China, Russia, India, Japan, the EU, and ASEAN etc. would likely play more significant roles in deciding when a real multi-polar world can be shaped. Presumably, the next ten to twenty years will be a very crucial period to see what type of global system can be forged.

Conclusion

This chapter has assessed the relevance of the Ukraine issue to great power relations and beyond. It has begun by analysed the origins of the Ukraine crisis.

Then it has, from a historical perspective, reviewed the implementation of the U.S.-led Cold War policy toward Russia, and explored how the Ukrainian issue has gradually come to the central stage with the deepening of the U.S. Cold War policy in Europe.

Further, this research has mainly focused on observing the possible social, economic, and strategic impacts of the Ukraine crisis on the main actors involved in the crisis including the U.S., Russia, the EU, and Ukraine. Apparently, the EU, Russia, and Ukraine have so far suffered more losses in various terms, and will likely continue to remain so if the Ukraine crisis cannot be contained at an earlier date. More severe consequences of the crisis might take a longer-time to come on to the surface.

Finally, this chapter has attempted to seek a proper means for helping the parties involved get out of the current crisis, and more crucially from a long-term strategic perspective, for making them adopt more inclusive and effective approaches to engage with each other.

In addition to that, by bearing the key strategic objectives of the concerned parties in mind, the final section has also tended to foresee the evolving trend of the Ukraine crisis by outlining a couple of possible scenarios, and further to understand how the different type of scenarios could have a relevance to the strategies of the major parties as well as to the possible shaping of a new European order and beyond.

There will be full of uncertainties and possibilities in the years ahead. Major powers and entities having been listed in this study would presumably matter more significantly in affecting the evolving trend of the global system.

Notes

1. Morelli L. Vincent, "Ukraine: Current Issues and U.S. Policy", *Congressional Research Service*, RL33460, 3 January 2017.
2. Ibid.
3. Ibid.
4. Archick Kristin and Mix E. Derek, "U.S.-EU Cooperation on Ukraine and Russia", *Congressional Research Service,* IN10129, 13 March 2015.
5. Morelli L. Vincent, "Ukraine: Current Issues and U.S. Policy", *Congressional Research Service,* RL33460, 3 January 2017.
6. Ibid.
7. Ibid.
8. Ibid, P31.
9. "Merkel Doubles down on Ukraine Peace Revelations", *RT*, 28 December 2022, https://www.rt.com/news/569036-merkel-minsk-accords-ukraine/
10. Rumer Eugene and Sokolsky Richard, "Thirty Years of U.S. Policy toward Russia: Can the Vicious Circle Be Broken?", *Carnegie Endowment,* 20 June 2019.
11. Cited from Rumer Eugene and Sokolsky Richard, "Thirty Years of U.S. Policy toward Russia: Can the Vicious Circle Be Broken?", *Carnegie Endowment*, 20 June 2019.
12. Ibid.
13. Ibid.
14. Ibid.
15. Ibid.
16. Fischer Sabine, "The EU and Russia: Conflict and Potentials of a Difficult Partnership", *SWP Research Paper,* German Institute for International and Security Affairs, January 2007.
17. Ibid.
18. Ibid.
19. Ibid.
20. Ibid, P14-15.
21. Ibid, P15.
22. Ibid, P15.
23. Ibid, P9.
24. Dragneva Rilka and Wolczuk Kataryna, "Russia, the Eurasian Customs Union and the EU: Cooperation, Stagnation or Rivalry?", Briefing Paper,

Chatham House*, August 2012.

25. Ibid.

26. Ibid.

27. Ibid.

28. Ibid, P10.

29. Cited from Dragneva Rilka and Wolczuk Kataryna, "Russia, the Eurasian Customs Union and the EU: Cooperation, Stagnation or Rivalry?", Briefing Paper, *Chatham House,* August 2012, P12.

30. Ibid.

31. Ibid, P13.

32. Rumer Eugene and Sokolsky Richard, "Thirty Years of U.S. Policy toward Russia: Can the Vicious Circle Be Broken?", *Carnegie Endowment,* 20 June 2019.

33. Ibid.

34. Ibid.

35. Archick Kristin and Mix E. Derek, "U.S.-EU Cooperation on Ukraine and Russia", *Congressional Research Service*, IN10129, 13 March 2015.

36. Ibid.

37. Ibid.

38. Morelli L. Vincent, "Ukraine: Current Issues and U.S. Policy", *Congressional Research Service,* RL33460, 3 January 2017, P37.

39. Ibid, P35.

40. Archick Kristin and Mix E. Derek, "U.S.-EU Cooperation on Ukraine and Russia", *Congressional Research Service*, IN10129, 13 March 2015.

41. Morelli L. Vincent, "Ukraine: Current Issues and U.S. Policy", *Congressional Research Service*, RL33460, 3 January 2017.

42. Ibid.

43. Ibid.

44. Ibid.

45. Ibid.

46. Council of the European Union, "Timeline - EU Response to Russia's Invasion of Ukraine", https://www.Consilium.europa.eu/en/policies/eu-response-ukraine-invasion/timeline-eu-response-ukr aine-invasion

47. Ibid.

48. Ibid.

49. Ibid.

50. Council of the European Union, "Infographic - How Much Gas Have the EU Countries   Stored?",

https://www.consilium.europa.eu/en/infographics/gas-storage-capacity/

51. "Europe's Imports of Russian LNG Increase by 42% in 2022, Report Suggests",https://sputniknews.com/20221129/europes-imports-of-russian-lng-increase-by-42-in-2022-report-su ggests-1104807087.html

52. Elena Mazneva and Anna Shiryaevskaya, "EU Is Hooked on Russia LNG", *Bloomberg,*
https://www.rigzone.com/news/wire/eu_is_hooked_on_russia_lng-30-nov-2022-171221-article/

53. Council of the European Union, "Timeline - EU Response to Russia's Invasion of Ukraine", https://www.consilium.europa.eu/en/policies/eu-response-ukraine-invasion/timeline-eu-response-ukr aine-invasion/

54. "OPEC Maintains Oil Targets amid Uncertainty over Russian Sanctions", *CBS News,* 4 December, 2022, https://www.cbsnews.com/news/opec-oil-production-russia-sanctions/

55. O'keefe Ed and Quinn Melissa, "Biden Administration Asks Congress for $32.5 billion for COVID and Ukraine", *CBS News,* 4 March 2022, http://www.cbsnews.com/news/ukraine-aid-biden-administration-cong ress-covid/

56. The White House, "Fact Sheet on U.S. Security Assistance for Ukraine", 16 March2022, http://www.whitehouse.gov/briefing-room/statements releas es/2022/03/16/fact-sheet-on-u-s-securit y-assistance-for-ukraine/

57. Semler Bystephen, "The Ukraine Aid Bill Is A Massive Windfall for U.S. Military Contractors", 26 May 2022, http://www.jaco binmag.com/2 022/05/ukraine-aid-bill-congress-biden-military-health

58. Lori Robertson, "U.S. Aid to Ukraine, Explained", 2 December 2022, https://www.factcheck.org/2022/12/u-s-aid-to-ukraine-explained/

59. Dabrowski Marek et al., "Ukraine: Trade Reorientation from Russia to the EU", 13 July 2020, http://www.bruegel.org/2020/07/ukraine-trade-reorientation-from-russia-to-the-eu/

60. Morelli L. Vincent, "Ukraine: Current Issues and U.S. Policy", *Congressional Research Service*, RL33460, 3 January 2017.

61. Ibid.

62. For the number of death caused by the COVID-19 pandemic in Ukraine, data cited by this study was till 6 December 2022, https://www.w orldometers.info/coronavirus/country/ukraine/

63. Vidyashree S, "Ukraine Economy to Shrink by 45.1% in 2022, Russia's GDP to Drop by 11.2%: World Bank", *Republicworld,* 11 April 2022, http://www.republicworld.com/world-news/russia-ukraine-crisis/ukraine-

economy-to-shrink-by-45-do t-1-percent-in-2022-russias-gdp-to-drop-by-11-dot-2-percent-world-bank-articleshow.html; Also see "IMF Forecasts Decline in Ukraine's GDP by 35%", *Interfax,* 19 April 2022, http://interfax.com/newsroom/top-stories/78378/

64. "The War Cost the Ukrainian Economy $600 billion", *TxT,* 19 April 2022, https://www.txtreport.com/news/2022-04-19-the-war-cost-the-ukrainian-economy-%24-600-billion.rJ ANBosVq.html

65. "Russia Issues New Estimate of Ukrainian Combat Losses", *RT,* https://www.rt.com/russia/567764-russia-ukraine-combat-losses/

66. "Where We Are Now: 100 Days of Crisis in Ukraine", *UNHCR*, http://www.unrefugees.org/news/where-we-are-now-100-days-of-crisis-in-ukraine/

67. "Number of Border Crossings between Ukraine and the Countries Selected, alongside the Russia-Ukraine War between 24 February and 29 November 2022 (in 1,000s)", *Statista*, https://www.statista.com/statistics/1293403/cee-ukrainian-refugees-by-country/

68. Ibid.

69. Rumer Eugene and Sokolsky Richard, "Thirty Years of U.S. Policy toward Russia: Can the Vicious Circle Be Broken?", *Carnegie Endowment,* 20 June 2019.

70. "Russia Continues to Diversify the Economy", *Credinform,* 4 May 2018, http://credinform.ru/en-GB/Publications/Herald/8fd8420dda03

71. Stockholm Institute of Transition Economics, "What Are the Effects of Banning Russian Oil and Gas across the EU?", 29 April 2022, https://www.hhs.se/en/about-us/news/site-publications/2022/what-are-the-effects-of-banning-russia n-oil-and-gas-across-the-eu/

72. European Commission, "EU Trade Relations with Russia", http://policy.trade.ec.europa.eu/eu-trade-relationships-country-and-region/countries-and-regions/rus sia_en

73. Russell Martin, "U.S.-Russia Relations - Geopolitical, Security, Economic, and Human Dimensions", *European Parliamentary Research Service,* https://www.europarl.europa.eu/RegData/etudes/BRIE/2022 /698919/EPRS_BRI(2022)698919_EN.pdf

74. Vidyashree S, "Ukraine Economy to Shrink by 45.1% in 2022, Russia's GDP to Drop by 11.2%: World Bank", *Republicworld,* 11 April 2022, http:/www.republicworld.com/world-news/russia-ukraine-crisis/ukraine-economy-to-shrink-by-45-dot-1-percent-in-2022-russias-gdp-to-drop-by-

11-dot-2-percent-world-bank-articleshow.html

75. "Russia: Inflation rate from September 2021 to October 2022 (compared to the same month of the previous year) '', *Statista,* http://www.statis ta.com/statistics/276323/monthly-inflation-rate-in-russia/

76. "US Reveals Value of Frozen Russian Assets", *RT,* https://www.rt.com/ business/558076-frozen-russian-assets-amount-revealed/

77. European Commission, "EU Trade Relations with Russia", http://policy. trade.ec.europa.eu/eu-trade-relationships-country-and-region/countries-and-regions/rus sia_en

78. The Diplomatic Service of the European Union, "Facts and Figures about EU-Russia Relations", July 2021, http://www.eeas.europa.eu/sites/ default/files/eeas-eu-russia_relation-en_2021-07.pdf

79. Stockholm Institute of Transition Economics, "What Are the Effects of Banning Russian Oil and Gas across the EU?", 29 April 2022, https://www.hhs.se/en/about-us/news/sitepublications/2022/what- are-the-effects-of-banning-russia n-oil-and-gas-across-the-eu/

80. Ibid.

81. Ibid.

82. Ibid.

83. "Closing Price of Brent, OPEC Basket, and WTI Crude Oil at the Beginning of Each Week from 2 March 2020 to 28 December 2022 (in U.S. dollars per barrel)", *Statista,* https://www.statista.com/statistics/326017/weekly-crude-oil-prices/

84. Ibid.

85. "U.S. and 30 Countries Commit to Release 60 Million Barrels of Oil from Strategic Reserves to Stabilize Global Energy Markets", 1 March 2022, https://www.energy.gov/articles/us-and-30-countries-commit-release-60-million-barrels-oil-strategic-r eserves-stabilize

86. Addy Bink, "How Much Oil Will Be Left in the US Strategic Reserve after Biden's Release?", *NewsNation,* 31 March 2022, https://www.newsnat ionnow.com/us-news/how-much-oil-will-be-left-in-the-us-strategic-reserve-after-bidens-release/

87. Ramon Padilla, "Where Are the US Strategic Oil Reserves? Here's How Many Barrels Remain and Where They Are", *USA TODAY,* 21 October 2022, https://www.usatoday.com/in-depth/graphics/2022/10/19/how-long-us-oil-reserves-last-size-supply-a mid-record-low/10541808002/

88. Addy Bink, "How Much Oil Will Be Left in the US Strategic Reserve after

Biden's Release?", *NewsNation,* 31 March 2022, https://www.newsna tionnow.com/us-news/how-much-oil-will-be-left-in-the-us-strategic-reserve-after-bidens-release/

89. Ibid.

90. "Monthly Natural Gas Price Index Worldwide from January 2020 to October 2022", *Statista,* https://www.statista.com/statistics/130 2994/monthly-natural-gas-price-index-worldwide/

91. Ibid.

92. "Europe's Imports of Russian LNG Increase by 42% in 2022, Report Suggests",https://sputniknews.com/20221129/europes-imports-of-russian-lng-increase-by-42-in-2022-report-su ggests-1104807087.html

93. Ramon Padilla, "As Global Oil Production Is Reduced, Will Gas Prices Increase or Decrease? The Answer Is Mixed", *USA TODAY*, 20 October 2022, https://www.usatoday.com/in-depth/graphics/2022/10/19/oil-pro duction-reduction-gas-prices-graph ics/10478122002/

94. "Liquefied Natural Gas (LNG) Exports from the United States from 2018 to 2022, with A Forecast Until 2023", *Statista,* https://www.stat ista.com /statistics/1099336/us-liquefied-natural-gas-exports/

95. Morelli L. Vincent, "Ukraine: Current Issues and U.S. Policy", *Congressional Research Service,* RL33460, 3 January 2017, P5.

96. Ibid, P8.

97. The Diplomatic Service of the European Union, "Facts and Figures about EU-Russia Relations", July 2021, http://www.eeas.europa.eu/sites/defa ult/files/eeas-eu-russia_relation-en_2021-07.pdf

98. Ibid.

99. Ibid.

100. Kissinger Henry, "Henry Kissinger's speech at the World Economic Forum in Davos", *Ukrainian Institute of Strategies of Global Development and Adaptation*, 26 May 2022, https://uisgda.com/en/rech-genri-kissindzhera -na-vsemirnom-ekonomicheskom-forume-v-davose.htm l

101. "Time for Ukraine talks 'not right now' - White House", *RT,* https://ww w.rt.com/news/568398-sullivan-ukraine-talks-russia/

CHAPTER 4

How Would the ASEAN Way Likely Affect the Forging of An Indo-Pacific Order and beyond?

On 8 August 1967, five Southeast Asian states consisting of Indonesia, Malaysia, the Philippines, Singapore, and Thailand in Bangkok jointly signed the Bangkok Declaration to mark the founding of the Association of Southeast Asian Nations (ASEAN). More than five decades on, ASEAN has achieved remarkably in driving regional integration, promoting institutional building, and managing intra-ASEAN and extra-ASEAN relations. By the late 1990s, the total number of the organization's member states had been extended to ten by subsequently including Brunei Darussalam, Burma (Myanmar), Cambodia, Laos, and Vietnam into the grouping in addition to the five founding members.

Since its formation, ASEAN, in comparison to a number of organizations, has generally adapted itself well to numerous changes at both regional and international levels, and managed to make the organization remain closely relevant to today's world.

Due to the great progress made by ASEAN in a number of fields, some observers took it as one of the most successful grouping in the world. Then, what has been the major driving force behind the organization's success? Some asserted that ASEAN's achievements cannot be separated from its member states' constant efforts in developing as well as in adhering to a unique ASEAN approach, namely the ASEAN Way, which is mainly characterized by respect for sovereignty, non-interference, consultation- and consensus-based decision making, and the application of peaceful means in setting disputes and so on.

Meanwhile, there are also different voices raised regarding the ASEAN Way - while accrediting the significance of the ASEAN Way, over the past years, in promoting regionalism and regional integration in both normative and pragmatic means, some argued that the ASEAN Way somehow has curbed ASEAN from addressing more contentious matters such as traditional security issue in the region as well as human rights issue within the member states of the organization.[1] Besides that, in facing the new historical context, some observers, from the economic perspective, presented a view that the ASEAN Way could affect ASEAN in pursuing a more advanced form of regional integration.[2]

Currently, the United States, in order to keep its relevance in the Indo-Pacific region, has developed a new strategy, namely the Indo-Pacific strategy, to re-engage with Asia. In the meantime, other major powers and entities in the Indo-Pacific region including ASEAN itself, China, Japan, and India have also been in the process of formulating and implementing their agendas.

Under these circumstances, how would ASEAN possibly respond to the uncertainties and challenges lying ahead, and whether the ASEAN Way could still work in managing a more complex regional environment?

This chapter aims to explore the linkage between the ASEAN Way and the possible forging of a new regional order in the Indo-Pacific region and beyond.

It will begin by observing and analysing the historical and cultural context of the shaping of the ASEAN Way. Then, it will assess in more details of what ASEAN has achieved by adhering to the ASEAN Way from a variety of dimensions, as well as of the challenges faced by ASEAN in sustaining the ASEAN Way, and how ASEAN could manage to overcome them. Finally, by taking the strategic intentions and objectives of the major powers into account, this project will tend to observe how ASEAN's engagements with the main stakeholders in the Indo-Pacific including India, Japan, China, and the United States would likely affect the prospect of the shaping of a new regional order in the Indo-Pacific region and beyond.

1. Cultural and Historical Context of ASEAN and of the ASEAN Way

It is assumed that historical events, culture, customs, and religious elements etc. all had ever played a role in directing Southeast Asian countries to form an organization like ASEAN, as well as in affecting the incremental shaping of the ASEAN Way. After having endured numerous ups and downs in history, the founding of ASEAN was reflective of the aspiration of Southeast Asian nations in fighting for self-determination and the identity of Southeast Asia. It was also an indication of Southeast Asian states' attempt to strengthen their collective capacity, by relying on which, to protect the interest of Southeast Asian states on the one hand, and to jointly contribute to regional peace, stability, and prosperity on the other hand.

1.1 Cultural linkage

Some observers tend to link the ASEAN Way with a Malay culture, which can be traced to an old tradition regarding how decisions were made in the small villages of some Southeast Asian countries such as Malaysia, Brunei, and Indonesia etc. The decision-making process took the form of inviting heads or representatives of the families living in the villages or countrysides to village gatherings/meetings, through which, to jointly find solutions for the problems commonly faced by the villages. All the representatives tended to deliberately exhibit an agreeable manner. Even when some of them strongly disagreed with each other on certain issues, they still preferred to voice their concerns carefully with a sensible or humorous manner.[3]

Apparently, this old Malay cultural tradition till nowadays still has a big influence to certain parts of Southeast Asia; and it still significantly affects how ASEAN tends to deal with its various partners.

In addition, from a broader cultural perspective, other parts of the Asian culture including the Chinese culture and the Indian culture in ancient times had already greatly influenced the societies of Southeast Asia. Throughout the earlier centuries long before the colonial period, Southeast Asians had started to practise merchandise trade with the people from other regions such as East Asia, South Asia, and the Middle

East. The ancient routes set for trade activities had also greatly facilitated the development and exchanges in other variety of areas including the cultural spectrum. Hence, in ancient times, Southeast Asia was already a region with rich cultural and religious diversities.[4]

Given China's commercial and cultural influence to Asia and beyond for a long historical period in ancient times, the Chinese Confucian and Taoist culture by then had generated a great impact on the countries and regions surrounding China including Southeast Asia.[5] There were no clearly divided borders between China and its Southeast Asian neighbours in old times. With the development of merchandise trade and of other kinds of exchanges between China and Southeast Asia, a significant number of Chinese people had moved to Southeast Asia and settled there permanently in ancient times.[6] Nowadays, ethnic Chinese people constitute a very large proportion of Southeast Asian population. Apparently, China and Southeast Asia had started to build connectivity since the very earliest ages in history. The ancient Chinese values and culture advocating for peace and harmony were compatible with the old local tradition and culture of Southeast Asian states; and the mixture or integration of them, in modern times, had crucially affected how the unique ASEAN approach had been shaped.

1.2 Historical Context

From a historical perspective, It is generally believed that what had happened from the colonial period to the end of the Cold War in Southeast Asia had played the most significant part in leading to the formation of ASEAN. In contrast to the cultural influence to the shaping of the ASEAN approach, the historical dimension had very much impacted on the establishment of ASEAN and the forging of the ASEAN Way in a negative way. In other words, a few centuries of catastrophes and conflicts ever happened in Southeast Asia, and in the meantime the repercussions and grievances endured by the small powers in this region had finally pushed them to find a most appropriate and effective solution to restore and sustain peace, and to better protect their sovereignty, national identity, and economic interests.

The colonial period had roughly begun from the late 15th and the beginning of the 16th century. By then, the Asian regions generally were more advanced and prosperous in material, technical, scientific, and technological terms. Long before the colonial era, Southeast Asia had started to have frequent exchanges with the regions adjacent to it, yet the exchanges between Southeast Asia and other regions had mostly focused on merchandise trade, and cultural and religious exchanges.

By the late 15th century, the advancement of seafaring technology motivated the western powers and companies to explore a broader and new outside world. Discoveries of new islands and the establishment of settlements thereafter in the newly discovered islands and continents across various parts of the globe marked the beginning of the colonial period. The colonial powers had very ambitious goals. They were roughly motivated by the interests in seeking raw materials and commercial profits, seizing territories, and seeking political, economic, social, cultural, and religious domination of the regions being colonized more broadly.[7]

1.2.1 Late 15th Century - Late 19th Century: the Emergence and Expansion of Colonialism

Following the Treaty of Tordesillas signed between Spain and Portugal in June 1494, Spain and Portugal firstly emerged as the oldest colonial powers. The treaty divided the world into two spheres for the two powers to explore - Spain took the western half and Portugal got the eastern half.[8] The time frame ranging from the late 15th century to the late 19th century was the most significant period for the expansion of colonialism.

As accompanied with colonial expansion, there was a growing competition for domination among colonial powers across various regions of the globe. With the competition among them getting intense, conflicts and wars had started to take place. For instance, Britain and France, as driven by their competition to take control of America, had fought for about 80 years from 1689 to 1763. There were also other series of wars among the colonial powers such as the English-Dutch war in the late 17th century, the Dutch-Portuguese war from 1602 to 1663, and the Dutch-Spanish war in 1646 for taking over the Spanish colony in the Philippines etc.[9]

In addition to the struggles among the colonial powers themselves, in the meantime, they had also been facing the constant resistance against colonization and colonial rules by the indigenous people in the colonies.

As a result of the endless wars and struggles among the colonial powers as well as between the colonies and the colonizers, the dominant status of the old colonial powers including the Portuguese, the Spanish, and the Dutch had gradually faded away, while the late comers such as Britain, France, the U.S., and Japan by the late 19th century had grown stronger. The British expansionism had peaked by the late 19th and the beginning of the 20th century by possessing the largest size of lands across the globe.

As for the colonization process in Southeast Asia, it had generally followed the similar traits as the evolving process of colonial expansion at the global level. Portuguese, Spanish, and the Dutch were the earliest explorers to Southeast Asia. Portugal firstly established settlement in the region in 1511.[10] In the following few centuries, other colonial powers including Britain, France, Japan, and the United States had subsequently reached Southeast Asia and established bases there. Alongside the colonial expansion process, the competition for domination between the old colonial powers and the new comers to Southeast Asia, as well as the struggles between the indigenous residents and the colonial powers were getting intense. For instance, the Burmanese resistance against British annexation and colonization had lasted for more than 60 years from 1826 to 1888.[11]

By the late 19th century, the influence of the new colonial powers had surpassed that of the old ones. The dominant status of Britain and of France in Southeast Asia had been particular consolidated by then.

1.2.2 Late 19th Century - End of WWII: Colonial Expansion, Imperialism, and End of the Colonial Rule

By the end of the 19th century, colonial expansion had entered a new phase, namely the imperialist stage. For the situation in Southeast Asia, from the late 19th century to the end of WWII, conflicts and wars were still a major factor in affecting the relationship among imperial powers and between the imperialists and the local residents in this region. On the one hand, the struggles for seeking control in resources, capital, and markets among the imperial powers had kept growing; and on the other hand, a few centuries of domination and colonization by the colonial powers in Southeast Asia hadn't stopped the indigenous people's resistance against foreign domination.

A range of wars that had significantly altered the balance of imperial power structure in Southeast Asia and beyond mainly included the Spanish-American war happened in 1898 and the two World Wars in the first half of the 20th century.

Following the American-Spanish war, the U.S. replaced Spain's status to become the new colonizer of the Philippines. Afterward, the war of the Philippines's resistance against the U.S. recolonization was erupted. The war had lasted for about 10 years, and resulted in the death of around 400,000 to 600,000 Filipinos and of 10,000 Americans.[12]

As for the status of an Asian imperial power, Japan, during the second half of the 19th century, as driven by a series of reform policies adopted by the Japanese Meiji emperor, within a few decades, the country had quickly grown to an influential power in Asia, which motivated Japan to compete with the traditional colonial powers for supremacy, and further to replace their positions in Southeast Asia, as guided by Japan's ambition of building a "Greater East Asian Co-prosperity Sphere".[13] The escalation of tension between Japan and western powers plus the Japanese aggressive invasion against other Asian powers in East and Southeast Asia ultimately led to a full scale breaking out of WWII in the Pacific theater.

After all, a series of devastating wars and conflicts throughout the late 19th century to the middle of the 20th century had completely altered the global power structure. The end of WWII symbolized the ending of the European powers-dominated colonial period. Meanwhile, the Soviet Union and the United States had risen to the top. As a consequence of the huge losses of the traditional colonial powers like France and Britain during the two World Wars, besides the endless struggles against colonial ruling by indigenous Southeast Asians, the traditional colonial powers had lost the capacity and resources to maintain their status and influence in Southeast Asia. Therefore, by the end of the second World War, history had opened a new window for small Southeast Asian powers. After about four and a half centuries' of struggles against foreign domination in their political, economic, social, cultural, and religious affairs, most of the Southeast powers, within a decade after WWII, had subsequently managed to regain national independence - British Burma achieved national independence in 1948, the Philippines in 1946, Indonesia in 1949, and Cambodia, Laos, and Vietnam the three in 1953.[14]

1.2.3 Middle of the 20th Century - End of the Cold War: Ideological

Difference Becoming A Major Cause of Conflicts

After WWII, with colonial ruling in Southeast Asia gradually fading away, a number of Southeast Asian nations regained national independence. It was supposed to have opened a new chapter for Southeast Asia. Nevertheless, shortly after the end of WWII, the world had entered into a period of the Cold War, which was driven by the ideological confrontation between the U.S.-led capitalist camp and the Soviet Union-led socialist bloc. Southeast Asia had been dragged into a new type of great power confrontation. Some of them had failed to avoid becoming part of a series of ideology-driven conflicts. By then, proxy war led by great powers became a new phenomenon.

Against this background, a normal territorial dispute between any two of the Southeast Asian states could be pulled into the overall context of ideological confrontation between great powers. The major devastating wars having taken place related to Southeast Asia during the Cold War era included the *Konfrontasi* (Confrontation) between Malaysia and Indonesia during the 1960s, the first Indochina war between France and Vietnam, the second Indochina war between the U.S. and Vietnam, also known as the Vietnam War, and the third Indochina war between Vietnam and Cambodia.[15]

The *Konfrontasi* between Indonesia and Malaysia

The *Konfrontasi* was caused by the territorial dispute between Indonesia and Malaysia over the status of Northern Borneo. This was partially also a problem left by the western colonial ruling in the region. Throughout the colonial period, the northern part of Borneo was taken by the British, while the rest part of Borneo was under the control of the Dutch. In 1963, with Malaysia's declaration of independence from the British colonial ruling, Britain returned Northern Borneo to Malaysia. Indonesia and the Philippines strongly opposed that arrangement, as these two countries also claimed Northern Borneo. Then, following a referendum under the UN sponsorship, the people of Northern Borneo voted to join Malaysia ultimately. In response, both Indonesia and the Philippines didn't recognize the outcome of the referendum. A dispute and further a conflict between Indonesia and Malaysia broke out. By then, Indonesia under then President Sukano was supported by the Soviet Union and China, while Malaysia was under the sponsorship of

Australia, New Zealand, Britain, and the United States.[16]

Alongside the on-going *Konfrontasi* between Indonesia and Malaysia, a civil war in Indonesia had taken place in the meantime between then President Sukarno-led communist party and a military coup led by Suharto, who, under the great sponsorship of the U.S. and Britain in both financial and logistical terms, carried out nationwide killing against socialists and Sukarno-led communist party members. Throughout the Indonesian civil war from 1965 to 1967, around 500,000 to 1 million Indonesians had been persecuted by Suharto-led forces. The civil war ended with the victory of Suharto, which meanwhile led to the reconciliation between Indonesia and Malaysia in 1966.[17]

Some assumed that Indonesia's shift of direction away from the Soviet Union-led camp to the U.S.-led bloc, and the normalization of relationship between Indonesia and Malaysia paved the way for the founding of ASEAN.[18] Therefore, the establishment of ASEAN in August 1967 was believed by many as a response to the pressure to be possibly generated by communism. Nevertheless, in the Bangkok Declaration to mark the formation of ASEAN in 8 August 1967, this official document apparently expressed no intention of ASEAN to side with either of the two blocs; instead, it highlighted the significance of ASEAN in preserving Southeast Asian regional peace and stability and in promoting advancement in all other issue areas, in the spirit of equality and partnership, by abiding respect for justice and the rule of law, and in line with the principles of the United Nations Charter.[19]

The Bangkok Declaration also indicated that Southeast Asian countries "are determined to ensure their stability and security from external interference in any form or manifestation in order to preserve their national identities in accordance with the ideals and aspirations of their peoples."[20] In addition, this document affirmed that "all foreign bases are temporary and remain only with the expressed concurrence of the countries concerned, and are not intended to be used directly or indirectly to subvert the national independence and freedom of states in the area or prejudice the orderly processes of their national development."[21]

The ASEAN Declaration reflected the member states' intent to preserve the independent position of the organization in dealing with regional affairs and other major powers. However, in reality, as a result of the ideological confrontation between the great powers by then, ASEAN's stance on non-interference was very often compromised.

Therefore, it can be understood that, upon the formation of ASEAN, rhetorically the ASEAN Way from a certain degree was shaped, yet in practical and substantial terms, it had actually taken a much longer time for ASEAN to gradually cultivate, forge, and practise the ASEAN Way.

The Three Indochina Wars

In contrast to the situation in Indonesia, for the wars related to Vietnam, there was a different scenario. The socialist camp, over the conflicts happened in Vietnam, had managed to gain a big momentum in dealing with the U.S.- led camp.

During the first Indochina war between France and North Vietnam (South Vietnam by then was under the sponsorship of the U.S. in combat with North Vietnam) from 1946 to 1954, the U.S. had sided with France in fighting against North Vietnam, though the two countries had borne different purposes - the U.S. was motivated by an anti-communism rhetoric, while the French was intended to restore its colonial influence in the Indochina region. The war was ended with the victory of North Vietnam led by Ho Chi Minh's communist party. The outcome of the first Indochina war resulted in the convening of the Geneva Conference, which took place on 26 April 1954 in Switzerland.[22]

In line with the Geneva Accord reached on 20th July, France agreed to withdraw its forces; Vietnam would be divided into two parts, North Vietnam and South Vietnam, along the 17th Parallel; a general election would take place in both parts within two years on 20th July 1956 to decide which one, North Vietnam or South Vietnam, to unite and govern the whole country.[23]

The positive outcome generated by the Geneva Conference was that following the signing of the Geneva Accord, France pulled its forces out of Vietnam. However, the Geneva conference also revealed a very serious problem - which was that the U.S. and the government of South Vietnam were not ready to accept the result of the first Indochina war, as reflected by the fact that the U.S. and South Vietnam refused to sign on the Geneva Accord, even though they did admit the signing of the agreement by other parties.[24]

This problem planted the seed for the second Indochina war (Vietnam War) between the U.S. and North Vietnam to be taking place from 1954 to 1975.

Following the eruption of the Vietnam War, China and the Soviet

Union had also been involved in it by offering assistance to North Vietnam. The conflict had lasted for about two decades, ended in 1975, and culminated in the reunification of the country by the forces in North Vietnam, as well as the departure of the U.S. forces from Vietnam.

Some observers indicated that during the Vietnam War, the anti-war sentiments within the U.S. were getting higher and higher - the young people aged between 18 and 25 were strongly opposed the war in particular.[25] In addition to that, some within the U.S. also called for restraining the U.S. President authority to launch a war.[26] All these anti-war voices within the U.S. were assumed to have more or less contributed to the ending of the Vietnam War at an earlier date as well.

Shortly after the second Indochina war, on 24 February 1976, ASEAN held its first summit in Indonesia ever since the founding of the organization in 1967, leading to the signing of two important documents: the Treaty of Amity and Cooperation (TAC), and the ASEAN Concord.[27] Through the TAC, ASEAN highlighted a series of fundamental principles upheld by the organization including "mutual respect for independence, sovereignty, equality, territorial integrity, and national identity of all nations", "non-interference in the internal affairs of one another", and the "settlement of differences or disputes by peaceful means" and so on; while the ASEAN Concord outlined the terms related to economic cooperation and conflict resolution.[28]

These documents manifested another crucial step further made by ASEAN in forging the ASEAN Way.

The third Indochina war was broken out as a result of Vietnam's invasion of Cambodia in 1978. ASEAN and the major powers including the U.S., China, and the Soviet Union, in response, were strongly opposed the invasion. Under the pressure imposed by the major powers, in particular, China and the Soviet Union, Vietnam pulled its forces out of Cambodia.[29] After all, the end of WWII didn't bring peace and stability to Southeast Asia. During the Cold War, Southeast Asian nations had been greatly affected by the ideological confrontation between great powers. Nevertheless, throughout this period, they had made a significant and first step in finding a way to protect the interest of Southeast Asia, as reflected by the founding of ASEAN.

1.2.4 End of the Cold War - Present: the Shaping of the ASEAN Way Entering A Pragmatic Stage

After the Cold War, ideology was not the dominant factor anymore in affecting relations and cooperation among countries. The breaking down of the ideological wall meant a new beginning for ASEAN to reassess its position in regional affairs. Alongside the deepening of globalization and of regional integration since the 1990s, the development of ASEAN and the forging of the ASEAN Way have entered a more pragmatic stage.

In the aftermath of the Cold War, major powers were in a crucial period of adjusting their agendas. By then, due to the economic influence of the countries like the U.S. and Japan, ASEAN had maintained closer economic engagements with them. After the Asian financial crisis in 1997-1998, ASEAN's relations with China, especially in the economic aspect, had grown very rapidly. In response to the financial crisis, the moves taken by China such as insisting not to devalue its currency as well as offering assistance to Southeast Asian countries during that difficult time had made them perceive more positively of China's role in the region.[30]

Then, during the 2000s, a range of events including China's accession to the World Trade Organization, and the 2008 global financial crises etc. had driven the regional geo-economic pattern to undergo further changes. China's economic ties with ASEAN had been getting closer in the first decade of the new century.

In the early 2000s, following the 9.11 terrorist attacks, the U.S. had started to prioritize the implementation of its counter-terrorism strategy. Some observers preferred to see that the U.S. prioritization of conducting its counter-terrorism strategy as well as other range of policies related to the Middle East had left a space for ASEAN and China to grow their economic ties more rapidly throughout the same period.

In response to the 2008 global financial crises, the Asian economies generally seemed to have performed better more or less. Then, in the aftermath of the global financial crises, the U.S. had carried out a "Return to Asia" strategy, through which, expecting to consolidate the U.S. ties, particularly from the security and economic dimensions, with Southeast Asian states.

The implementation of the U.S. strategy had affected the region in certain ways, especially, in relation to the security relations between China and individual Southeast Asian countries. Nevertheless, ASEAN's position generally wasn't affected by the U.S. strategy. The fact that ASEAN, in response to the external pressure, was able to adhere to its principles also manifested that the development of the organization and the practice of the ASEAN Way had made more substantial progress.

Since the 2010s, the regional and international environment has been undergoing further rapid changes. Against the background that the U.S. is in the process of planning and implementing its Indo-Pacific strategy, which, in contrast to the previous U.S. strategies, would be expected to generate a broader impact, the regional situation will likely become more complex.

Under this circumstance, from ASEAN's perspective, how would ASEAN deal with the possible challenges to be generated, alongside the implementation of various strategies by the major stakeholders in this region in the years ahead? How likely could the ASEAN Way be further practised and sustained? The next section of this chapter would aim to assess these issues. Before doing that, it would briefly outline and analyse some of the core achievements made by ASEAN since the end of the Cold War first.

2. Achievements & Challenges

2.1 Achievements Made by ASEAN through Practising the ASEAN Approach

ASEAN has managed to make significant achievements in driving regional economic integration, promoting regional political inclusiveness, and developing a range of frameworks to facilitate regional connectivity.

More specifically, from the economic dimension, ASEAN has made a great progress in facilitating regional economic cooperation and connectivity together with the organization's key dialogue partners. To better regulate ASEAN's relations with its dialogue partners, it has developed a unique ASEAN model, known as the "ASEAN Plus", which on the one hand weighs ASEAN's central role; and on the other hand highlights the importance of ASEAN's connection with its dialogue partners. The extension and evolution of the "ASEAN Plus" model in the economic field has led to the forging of a range of free trade cooperation mechanisms including the Regional Comprehensive Economic Partnership Agreement (RCEP), which is expected to play a crucial part in continuing to drive regional economic cooperation and integration.

From the political aspect, throughout the 1980s to the 1990s, ASEAN had accepted five new members, two of which - Vietnam and Laos - have a different political governance system from other members of the organization. This move taken by ASEAN can be a very crucial step in substantially making ASEAN a more inclusive and neutral organization. It consolidated the organization's position, greatly contributed to regional inclusiveness and confidence building, and was conducive to ASEAN's efforts in promoting regional peace and stability.

With regard to institutional building and the formation of a set of frameworks, over the past years, ASEAN has developed a range of ASEAN-led multilateral mechanisms consisting of the ASEAN Plus Three, East Asia Summit (EAS), ASEAN Regional Forum (ARF), and ASEAN Defence Ministers' Meeting Plus (ADMM+), etc. These series of frameworks have served as good platforms for ASEAN and the stakeholders, which have a relevance to the region, to jointly find solutions for the common challenges faced by them.

Overall, the past decades, since the founding of ASEAN, have been a process for the organization to make constant efforts to develop a unique approach that is most suitable to ASEAN. They have also been a process for ASEAN to make progress step by step in a number of areas by relying on the ASEAN approach. Over the past years, the ASEAN Way has generally served the organization's mission well in helping maintain regional peace, stability, and economic progress. Then, in the years ahead, what would be the major challenging issues for ASEAN to deal with? How likely could the ASEAN Way continue to serve the interest of the organization, and of the Indo-Pacific region?

2.2 Challenges & Arguments in Relation to the Application of the ASEAN Way

As usual, in the coming years, ASEAN would continue to face both external and internal challenges. The external challenges, as already mentioned, would mainly derive from the implementation of various strategies by the main actors which have a close relevance to this region; while the internal challenges would be primarily caused by the intra-ASEAN engagements.

One of the issues raised concerning the function of the ASEAN approach is about the implications of the ASEAN Way to intra-ASEAN integration. Some assumed that the ASEAN Way, under the current situation, could affect the further improvement of intra-ASEAN integration. Over the past years, ASEAN has made a great progress in promoting regional integration and developing regional connectivity together with various partners, yet the intra-ASEAN trade and economic integration has so far lagged behind the ideal progress as some have expected. For instance, the share of intra-ASEAN trade out of ASEAN's total trade volume had only secured a marginal growth from 22% in 2000 to 24% in 2015, in contrast to 64% for intra-EU trade out of the EU's total.[31] Besides that, despite that the tariffs in intra-ASEAN trade have been cut to a very low level, yet the non-tariff barriers have further increased, as reflected by the fact that the tariff rates in average were down from 8.9% in 2000 to 4.5% in 2015, yet the non-tariff barriers rose from 1634 to 5975 through the same period.[32]

Obviously, the non-tariff barriers set by individual ASEAN members have played a big role in affecting the progress of intra-ASEAN economic integration. To address this issue, some argued that there is a need for ASEAN to exercise a certain degree of control such as taking more effective measures toward its members. Nevertheless, the non-interference and consensus-based "soft" approach of ASEAN has prevented the organization from adopting tougher measures to push its member states to alter their trade policies and practices.

Moreover, apart from the challenges faced by ASEAN in intra-ASEAN economic integration, the principle of non-interference in the internal affairs of ASEAN member states upheld by the organization has affected ASEAN's capacity in dealing with more contentious matters such as human rights issue.

Then, how to understand the above internal and external challenges facing ASEAN, as well as the doubts raised about the applicability of the ASEAN approach upon certain occasions?

The shaping and practice of the ASEAN Way has gone through a long period of time already; and throughout this whole process, ASEAN has accumulated a great deal of experiences in managing complex and critical intra-ASEAN and extra-ASEAN affairs. The ASEAN approach is not perfect, and it is still evolving, yet the ASEAN Way has so far proved to be the most appropriate and successful approach in maintaining regional peace and stability in general terms.

Regional peace and stability is the foundation for promoting the development and advancement of all other areas of issues including achieving economic progress and building connectivity among all players in the region. Apart from that, the ASEAN approach has been very successful in setting a good example for promoting regional inclusiveness, as reflected by the fact that ASEAN has long been advocating the principle of equality among all its member states, regardless of the type of the ASEAN members' economic or political systems and of the size of their economies.

Some maintained that there is a need for ASEAN to adopt a more interventionist agenda in order to advance the level of regional integration, and to deal with more complex issues. Nevertheless, the interventionist approach having been carried out by external powers for about five centuries from the colonial period to the end of the Cold War hadn't brought peace, stability, and prosperity to Southeast Asia. Numerous examples happened in the past and taking place nowadays across various parts of the world proved that the interventionist approach, in particular, military intervention can only make the conflict situation get worse. Under these circumstances, there is no reason to believe that an interventionist approach would achieve better outcomes than the current ASEAN Way.

Therefore, to manage the external challenges to be possibly generated by various conflicting interests of the main players in the region, the ASEAN Way should still be the most appropriate approach in protecting ASEAN's interest on the one hand, and in dealing with ASEAN's relations with major powers on the other hand.

ASEAN, through a series of documents, has tended to highlight the significance of ASEAN Centrality. To sustain the ASEAN Way and to enhance the central role of ASEAN, it is in need for ASEAN to position itself as a more significant mediator or coordinator in the complicated regional and international affairs. The ASEAN Way has actually already put ASEAN in a better position, in contrast to other main actors in the Indo-Pacific region, to play a coordinating or mediating role.

In relation to the issue that, compared to extra-ASEAN economic and trade practices, less progress has been made over the past years in intra-ASEAN trade, there might be a lot of reasons behind this. Non-tariff barriers obviously have been one of the factors in affecting intra-ASEAN trade practices.

Non-tariff barrier is a common issue in today's trade practices. The more advanced and integrated economies such as the European Union, the United States, and Japan etc. have also long been troubled by it, due to which, trade negotiations among the more integrated economies have proved to be very tough and hardly to reach an agreement within a short period as well. Therefore, the ASEAN Way is not the major cause in affecting the pace of integration among ASEAN members.

The diversity in the level of development among ASEAN member states could also be an important factor, which should be taken into account, when it relates to assessing the pace of intra-ASEAN integration.

Anyway, to deal with the matter of non-tariff barriers in intra-ASEAN trade, some suggested that the ASEAN Secretariat needs to play a bigger role by making itself an "operating system" to help facilitate cohesive and effective policy-making among member states.[33] Besides that, the individual ASEAN members with a specific concern on relevant economic policies and regulatory constraints may try to see whether a bilateral approach rather than a multilateral approach could help settle the matter related to non-tariff barriers.

Compared with intra-ASEAN economic performance, the extra-ASEAN economic engagements have made a dramatic progress over the past decades. For example, during 1995-2016, India-ASEAN trade recorded an average annual growth rate of around 11.9%; and India's imports from and exports to ASEAN constituted an annual growth rate of 12.3% and of 11.4% in average respectively over the same period.[34] For China-ASEAN trade, the merchandise trade between China and ASEAN in 2020 stood at $516.9 billion, corresponding 24.7% of ASEAN's total foreign trade, surging from 15.3% in 2009.[35]

The above facts reflected that ASEAN would allow its members to have the flexibility to choose their cooperation partners in the broad Indo-Pacific region, which could better meet their needs. The matter of flexibility can be another advantage of the ASEAN model - the sovereign right of ASEAN's member states wouldn't be compromised by being a member of the organization.

In the new era, ASEAN has been set to play a central role among all its key dialogue partners. Hence, ASEAN's focus in promoting regional integration has already been beyond the Southeast Asian region. The ASEAN model is generally conducive to the facilitation and optimization of the interconnected supply chains from a wide spectrum in the Indo-Pacific.

Furthermore, with regard to the argument that the ASEAN Way

would limit ASEAN's capacity in addressing more contentious issues like human rights violations in its member states, given that numerous examples in history proved that a tough intervention approach had led to more disastrous consequences, there is a need for the relevant parties to jointly apply a more creative diplomatic approach to deal with disputable or conflicting matters in the future. For example, while letting ASEAN take a main position in helping mediate or consult with the conflicting parties within the member states, ASEAN may also need to take into account closely working with other international organizations such as the UN or with other major powers to jointly find a more appropriate and peaceful solution.

Over the past years, the process of shaping and practising the ASEAN Way has explicitly shown how ASEAN has interacted with both its member states and other various partners. Against the new historical background, it is assumed that the ASEAN approach would still have a big role to play in shaping the intra-ASEAN and extra-ASEAN relations from a variety of dimensions. The next section will tend to observe the evolving trends of ASEAN's engagements with its key dialogue partners consisting of India, Japan, China, and the U.S., as well as the impacts of the relevant interactions on the prospect of jointly forging an Indo-Pacific order.

3. The Evolving Trends of ASEAN's Engagements with Its Main Dialogue Partners & the Prospect of Shaping An Indo-Pacific Order and beyond

3.1 India and ASEAN

India became a key dialogue partner of ASEAN in 1996, and in 2012, the relationship between the two sides was upgraded to a Strategic Partnership.[36] Since the end of the Cold War, like other dialogue partners of ASEAN, India has subsequently joined a series of forums and frameworks led by ASEAN, such as the EAS, ARF, and ADMM Plus etc.

Over the past decades especially since India adopted an "Act East" policy upon the 12th ASEAN-India Summit and the 9th East Asia Summit in 2014,[37] India has taken its cooperative relationship with ASEAN as most significant to India in strategic terms. In other words, India considered its relationship with ASEAN as the "foundation" of its "Act East" policy,[38] or as a "cornerstone" of India's foreign policy in general terms.[39]

India, like other main actors in the region consisting of ASEAN, Japan, China, and the U.S., has designed its own Indo-Pacific vision. The "Act East" policy has been set at the centre of India's overall strategy in the Indo-Pacific region. India's decision to set ASEAN at the most significant position for the country reflected India's careful judgment and calibration from a wide variety of dimensions.

First, from the historical and cultural perspective, both India and the ASEAN countries are geographically located in Asia, and had ever been greatly influenced by the broad Asian culture and civilization in history. In ancient times, India and the small Southeast Asian powers had already had close exchanges; and both India and most of the Southeast Asian powers had been colonized by western powers. Therefore, they had shared the same grievances led by colonization. At a later stage in modern times, India and the Southeast Asian countries joined the Non-Aligned Movement, which somehow could have played a role in helping shape the ASEAN Way. Therefore, as being driven by the cultural linkages and the similar historical experiences between India and ASEAN states, India naturally feels closer to Southeast Asia.

Second, from the political and security aspect, the range of core principles such as non-interference and respect for sovereignty upheld and practised by ASEAN mean that ASEAN countries wouldn't likely cause a big threat to India in traditional security terms.

Third, in relation to the promotion of regional integration and the facilitation of regional networks, ASEAN by putting itself at the centre has created a wide range of networks and frameworks connecting the cooperation among the main actors that have a close relevance to the region. These series of mechanisms and networks have served as platforms not only for promoting the flow of ideas and knowledge in a variety of areas including economy and trade, social and cultural affairs, security, infrastructure, digital technology, supply chains, risk management, and climate change etc., but also for facilitating cooperation in substantial terms among various players in these areas. India, as one of the important actors in the Indo-Pacific, would expect to benefit from its participation in certain frameworks together developed with ASEAN from a long-term perspective.

Fourth, with regard to India-ASEAN economic cooperation, ASEAN has been a key partner of India in trade and investment. The current two-way merchandise trade between India and ASEAN is of around $80 billion on an annual basis,[40] making India the 6th largest trading partner of ASEAN. Meanwhile, India's foreign direct investment flowing into ASEAN amounted to $2.0 billion in 2019, making India the 8th largest source country for foreign direct investment in ASEAN among all ASEAN's dialogue partners.[41]

Apart from that, ASEAN is one of the most crucial and successful economic blocs in the world, with a potential for further expanding its influence against the backdrop that major powers would attach importance to the implementation of their Indo-Pacific visions in the years ahead. In addition, by taking the advancement of digital technology as a leverage, ASEAN would likely become one of the top five digital economies in the world. Therefore, by taking into account ASEAN's economic potential, as well as the advantage of geographical proximity between India and Southeast Asian countries, there is no reason for India not to attach significance to ASEAN.

Fifth, from a broad strategic perspective, India would likely prefer to cooperate more closely with ASEAN, rather than with other main actors like the U.S., China, and Japan, in order to better meet India's strategic interest in the Indo-Pacific.

The U.S. strategic intention is to include India as well as other allies of the U.S. into its. overall strategic arrangement in the Indo-Pacific region. Nevertheless, for India, being part of the U.S.- led agenda would risk compromising India's core interests. In addition, as an important advocate of the Non-Aligned Movement ever in history, India wouldn't easily give up its non-aligned position from a strategic perspective.

Not abandoning its non-aligned position doesn't mean that India would completely avoid cooperation with the U.S. on critical issues like security cooperation; mostly it means that India would take its strategic cooperation with the U.S. very carefully, should it affect India's core interest. In other words, India would try to keep its strategic autonomy under all circumstances.

India's case is different from that of another major power - Japan, given that Japan doesn't have enough defence capacity, and very much relies on the U.S. for protection. Ever since the end of WWII, Japan has made a great deal of efforts to raise Japan's profile at both the regional and international levels by expanding its economic power, and great achievements have been secured. Nevertheless, from the strategic perspective, Japan has still been significantly affected from occasion to occasion by the U.S. strategic adjustment.

Apparently, in contrast to Japan, India has more freedom to choose when it relates to security partners. Since India declared national independence in the late 1940s, strategically it has been able to keep its autonomy. Meanwhile, India has kept a close ties with Russia in many aspects including security cooperation. From the economic and trade perspective, India generally depends more on its economic ties with the partners, which are geographically adjacent to the country.

For China-India ties, the two countries border with each other, and are each other's important economic and trade partner. Both are emerging economies, and also the members of the BRICS grouping. From a certain sense, India and China would tend to defend the interests and voices of developing countries in the wide global community. Nevertheless, the relationship between them has appeared to be getting a bit more complicated, along with China's rising influence in recent years - on the one hand, China and India would like to see a closer economic ties between them, and they would have the intention, in line with their capacity, to jointly create certain global public goods; and on the other hand, India has been getting cautious about China's rising influence in the neighbourhood, as a result of which, India has tended to see China as a major potential threat. Besides that, the territorial dispute between the two countries has been a crucial issue waiting for the two sides to work out a more appropriate approach to manage.

Given the above circumstances, China, just like the U.S. and Japan, wouldn't likely be taken as the most ideal partner of India from India's perspective.

Overall, by taking all the above five major factors into account, India would take ASEAN, rather than the U.S., China, or Japan, as its most ideal and significant strategic partner to better meet India's interest from a long-term perspective. In other words, ASEAN would continue to be at the centre of India's foreign policy. The Indian side has already indicated that India is supportive of ASEAN Centrality, and that "a cohesive, responsive, and prosperous ASEAN is central to India's Indo-Pacific vision and India's 'Act East' policy, and contributes to security and growth for all in the region."[42]

In the meantime of designing a strategic agenda to better serve India's interest, there is also a need to see the challenges lying ahead in implementing such an agenda. Under the new situation, a very crucial issue for India to bear in mind should be related to what India and ASEAN can reciprocally offer each other, given that India would take ASEAN as the foundation of India's foreign policy and expect to benefit from a closer partnership with ASEAN.

In late 2019, India dropped out of the negotiation on the free trade agreement RCEP, which covers more than 2.2 billion global population and constitutes around 30% of the global GDP.[43] So far the ten ASEAN member states plus the five dialogue partners of ASEAN including South Korea, Japan, China, New Zealand, and Australia have signed the agreement. There could be a number of reasons to explain India's withdrawal from the RCEP negotiations, one of which could be related to the rising trade imbalances between India and most of the RCEP members. Over the past five to six years, India's trade deficits with the RCEP countries have almost doubled.[44]

Dropping out of the RCEP somehow also reflected that, instead of committing to a multilateral economic approach, India would much prefer to seek an alternative model to engage with ASEAN member states. India has already insinuated an interest in selectively deepening cooperation with individual ASEAN member countries through applying a trilateral or bilateral approach. For instance, to better facilitate the business connectivity between India and individual ASEAN member states, India has managed to make a great progress in carrying out the India-Myanmar-Thailand Trilateral Highway and the Kaladan Multimodal Project; and the Indian government currently is also taking into account extending this Trilateral Highway to Cambodia, Laos, and Vietnam.[45]

Meanwhile, concerning India's relevance to the RCEP, there may also be a need for India to understand that the economic relationship among economic entities is not only about trade figures, crucially it is also related to building and expanding economic connectivity, exchanging ideas and knowledge, and driving changes in a wide variety of areas beyond trade and economic activities - as one observer argued: "greater multidimensional economic connectivity increases the likelihood that an economy will absorb new ideas and increase long-run growth. Economic connectivity influences trade and investment, but it also results in [the] exchange [of] ideas, technology, and institutional arrangements, which are all potential sources for spillovers to growth and may indirectly influence shared prosperity."[46]

After all, it is assumed that promoting joint gains of India and ASEAN through whatever approaches - bilateral, trilateral, or multilateral - would not only serve the interests of both India and ASEAN states, but also would contribute to regional prosperity.

3.2 Japan and ASEAN

Japan is a significant economic partner, donor, and investor of ASEAN. As one of the key dialogue partners of ASEAN, Japan over the past decades has established close cooperation relationship with ASEAN in a number of areas covering economy and trade, traditional and nontraditional security, infrastructure, and social and cultural affairs etc.

The two-way trade between Japan and ASEAN reached $225.9 billion in 2019, while the FDI flowing from Japan to ASEAN amounted to $20.4 billion, making Japan the 4th largest trade partner of ASEAN, behind China, the United States, and the EU, and the 2nd biggest FDI source country for ASEAN after the United States.[47]

For a certain period of time, especially, during the 1980s and 1990s, Japan's economic power had ever secured a great deal of influence in Southeast Asia. Then, since the beginning of the 2000s, Japan's role in Southeast Asia had been relatively declining, along with China's growing influence in the region. So, Japan somehow sees China's rising connectivity with Southeast Asian countries as one of the major challenges to Japan's interest in the region.

For a few decades after WWII, Southeast Asian states had held a hostile stance toward Japan, and been very cautious about Japan's motivation in pursuing close engagements with the countries in the region. They had generally taken Japan's engagements with the region as an "economic invasion", and assumed that a resurgence of militarism could come later following the "economic invasion".[48]

In order to end the much isolated status of Japan in Asia, the Japanese then Prime Minister Fukuda Takeo paid a special visit to Southeast Asia in 1977. Upon his trip to the region, Fukuda delivered a speech in Manila, which was later commonly described as the Fukuda Doctrine, depicting the following key ideas - Japan would seek to engage with Southeast Asian countries through 'heart to heart' dialogue; Japan would not turn itself into a military power again; and Japan would treat ASEAN as an equal partner.[49]

From then on, the tension between Japan and Southeast Asian states had started to ease, and Japan's relationship with them had been step by step back on to normal. The Fukuda Doctrine had significantly contributed to the improvement and normalization of Japan's relations with ASEAN. In 1977, Japan and ASEAN formalized their diplomatic relations.

Roughly, the period ranging from the 1970s to the 1990s can be a golden era for the expansion of Japan's economic power in Asia and beyond. Japan's economic boom throughout this period cannot be separated from the growing connectivity between Japan and ASEAN in various terms.

From the economic and trade dimension, Japan's investment, technology, and official development assistance transferred to Southeast Asia had played a crucial role in helping the development process of Southeast Asian states. Meanwhile, the raw materials from Southeast Asia had met the demands of Japan's industrialization and helped sustain Japan's economic growth. Besides that, given the shortage of Japanese domestic labour forces, the large number of young population in Southeast Asia were very attractive to Japanese investors having businesses in the region. Further, the size of Southeast Asian population also meant an ideal consumer market for absorbing the Japanese products.[50]

From the geographic and geo-strategic perspective, the geographic location of Southeast Asia also serves Japan's strategic interest well. Southeast Asia is situated in a critical point linking the Pacific and Indian oceans. The Asian countries heavily rely on the sea lanes in this region for trading with other regions of the world including the Middle East. For instance, for Japan, around 85% of Japanese oil imports from the Middle East need to cross through Southeast Asian waters.[51] Therefore, obviously, the geographic location of Southeast Asia naturally carries a strategic significance to Asian countries including Japan.

By taking the above factors into account, Japan has long been taking Southeast Asia strategically important to Japan and been very active in seeking to build a close ties with the countries in the region. By doing so throughout the 1970s to the 1990s, Japan's industrialization process and the Japanese economy had benefited from its connectivity with Southeast Asia greatly.

Since the beginning of the new century, following China's entry into the WTO and the opening of the Chinese market to the outside world, China-ASEAN cooperation in all key areas, especially in relation to the economic and trade aspect has grown very rapidly. The rising connectivity between China and ASEAN, compared with the relative declining position of Japan in this region had made Japan sense a challenge caused by China. Therefore, for a certain period of time from around the mid-2000s to the mid-2010s in particular, Japan had taken China as a major potential challenger to Japan's interest in Southeast Asia, and started to subsequently adopted a series of polices and measures to deal with the increasing present of China in the region.

Domestically, Japan had taken a series of actions, in particular, related to the security aspect such as pushing for the amendment of Japanese constitution on the part of lifting the ban on the right of collective self-defence, raising Japan's defence budget, setting up a National Security Council, and nationalizing the Diaoyu Islands etc. Meanwhile, from the external perspective, Japan had prioritized the formulation and implementation of Japan's policies in accommodation with the relevant policy measures adopted by U.S. toward Asia including the U.S. "Pivot to Asia" strategy. The series of moves made by Japan roughly from the mid-2000s to the mid-2010s had led to a rising tension between Japan and China.

The set of measures taken by Japan through the period just mentioned above hadn't prevented China and ASEAN from growing closer. It is assumed that three core factors over the past years have contributed to the increasing ties between ASEAN and China, consisting of the ASEAN Way, the inter-connected industrial chains jointly facilitated by China and ASEAN countries, and the Declaration on Conduct of Parties in the South China Sea (DOC) in managing the territorial disputes between China and certain ASEAN countries (more detailed analysis regarding the three factors' relevance to the growing ties between China and ASEAN can be found in the later part of this chapter).

In the new era, against the background that the U.S. has set a new agenda toward Asia, Japan has also adjusted its strategy in the Indo-Pacific region, which, in contrast to the strategies adopted by Japan in the past, obviously carries a grander purpose of Japan. From the 1970s to the 1990s, the main purpose of Japan's engagement with ASEAN had reflected its attempt to meet Japan's interest in a narrower space. By then, as already mentioned, Japan was interested in the scale of the Southeast Asian market, the size of the population, natural resources in

Southeast Asia, as well as the geo-strategic location of the region. As for Japan's new strategy, it would take the Indo-Pacific region as a base, by depending on which, to expand Japan's reach beyond the Asian region.

In this regard, Southeast Asia, in line with Japan's Indo-Pacific strategy, would serve as a key strategic point linking Asia and other parts of the world; the ASEAN model and some of the successful experiences accumulated by ASEAN would be transferred to other regions of the world such as the Middle East and Africa etc. Japan's Indo-Pacific strategy was designed to be able to meet a broader and long-term interest of Japan.

By bearing the above grand purpose in mind, it appears that the ASEAN Way practised by the organization hasn't so far met Japan's needs well. From Japan's perspective, generally, the membership structure of ASEAN mixed with democracies and non-democracies, as well as the core principles upheld by the organization, have significantly affected ASEAN's decision-making process more in a way that may not be able to serve Japan's interest well in a long run. Therefore, Japan and Australia ever advocated forming an Asian Community with a more interventionist agenda, Nevertheless, ASEAN wasn't attracted to this idea.[52]

Japan has long been having an interest in bringing ASEAN into the orbit of the U.S.- led alliance system in more substantial terms, from which, Japan can benefit also. However, from ASEAN's perspective, joining the U.S.- led alliance system obviously counters the ASEAN Way, the core principles held by ASEAN, and the ASEAN Centrality. The essence of the ASEAN Centrality was designed to set ASEAN at the centre of a regional architecture, in line with which, ASEAN acts as a balancing force among the major powers to contribute to regional peace, stability, and economic progress in the Indo-Pacific. Losing the ASEAN Way and the ASEAN Centrality means the loss of the just cause for being a balancer. In that case, peace and stability in this region will not be sustained as well.

Therefore, in the years ahead, ASEAN will try to be committed to the ASEAN Way, as it has done over the past years. Upholding and practising the ASEAN Way is still assumed to be the most appropriate means not only to serve ASEAN's long-term interest, but also to contribute to the possible forging of an Indo-Pacific order and of a multi-polar world.

Upholding and enhancing the ASEAN Way doesn't mean an easy

path for ASEAN. It hasn't been easy, and will not be easy as well in the years ahead. The positive side of the matter is that ASEAN has already accumulated a lot of experiences over the past decades from the founding of the organization, and then the forging of the ASEAN Way more in rhetorical terms, to the cultivating and practising of the ASEAN Way in both rhetorical and substantial terms.

3.3 China and ASEAN

China and Southeast Asian states are close neighbours; and in the very early age of human history, they had already started to conduct commercial, social, cultural, and religious exchanges. From the colonial period to the end of WWII, China and Southeast Asian countries had suffered from the aggression of colonial powers and then of imperial powers. During the Cold War, due to ideological difference and Cold War pressure, China and some Southeast Asian nations, from certain sense, had missed the opportunity to develop closer.

The end of the Cold War opened a new beginning for them to develop a different type of relationship. Exchanges and cooperation between China and Southeast Asian countries in various areas had started to move up in the 1990s, yet the territorial disputes between China and a few Southeast Asian states somehow had affected China-ASEAN cooperation to grow more rapidly.

At the beginning of the new century, as driven by a series of new measures taken by China to further open up the Chinese market including joining the WTO, China and ASEAN in 2002 signed the Framework on Free Trade Agreement, which set a precondition for China-ASEAN cooperation in the economic and trade sphere to move up more smoothly and quickly. In the same year, the two sides also managed to reach an agreement on the Declaration on Conduct of Parties in the South China Sea for properly dealing with the territorial disputes between China and Southeast Asian countries. The series of actions jointly taken by China and ASEAN significantly paved the way for the flourish of China-ASEAN cooperation at a later stage.

Over the past decades, regional integration in the broad Asian region has made a dramatic progress, from which, countries in the region including China and Southeast Asian nations have greatly benefited. Nowadays China and ASEAN have developed an interdependent relationship in a number of areas; the economic and trade cooperation between the two sides has especially achieved a remarkable progress. Till 2022, China has been ASEAN's number one trade partner for 13 consecutive years already. Since 2020, ASEAN has replaced the U.S. and the EU to become China's largest trade partner. For the first seven months of 2022, China-ASEAN trade had amounted to USD 544.9 billion.[53] Apart from trade, China remains as the 4th largest foreign investor of ASEAN, with investment covering the sectors of telecommunication, finance, insurance, manufacturing, real estate, whole sale and retail, and construction etc.[54]

In addition to the great achievement made by China and ASEAN in the economic and trade area, the cooperation between them in other relevant fields such as political and security issues, social and cultural affairs, infrastructure development etc. has also made a tremendous progress. More precisely, the flourish of China-ASEAN economic and trade cooperation cannot be isolated from their mutual support to each other in other range of areas.

First, from the political dimension, China and ASEAN share the similar core diplomatic principles for managing regional and international affairs such as respect for state sovereignty, non-interference, as well as application of peaceful means in settling disputes etc. The adoption of these principles by both sides is based on the lessons learnt from history. In the new era, China is supportive of ASEAN in managing intra-ASEAN and extra-ASEAN affairs in line with the ASEAN Way, as well as of the ASEAN-led regional architecture on various issues.

Second, from the security perspective, both China and ASEAN attach great significance to peace and stability in the Indo-Pacific region. Compared with the major powers like the United States, which is far from Asia geographically, Asian powers including China and Southeast Asian states are generally more concerned about peace and stability in this region. For China, it can be a very important factor in affecting China's domestic stability and economic growth as well as progress on other range of issues. Southeast Asian countries are believed to have the similar concerns. Therefore, China and ASEAN share a common concern in jointly creating a peaceful and stable neighbourly environment to meet each other's interest.

In order to sustain peace and security, on the one hand, China has joined the ASEAN-led security mechanisms such as the ARF and the ADMM Plus; and on the other hand, China and ASEAN have moved up efforts to develop more effective and substantial measures to handle their bilateral security issues. For instance, as already briefly indicated, the signing of the DOC between China and ASEAN in 2002 as well as the implementation of it have played a very crucial role in helping address the territorial disputes between China and Southeast Asian states in the South China Sea. The proper management of the disputes between China and its Southeast Asian neighbours over the past years has set a precondition for China and ASEAN to promote deep cooperation in other areas. In addition to the DOC, for better handling their territorial disputes, China and ASEAN have engaged in the negotiation of reaching a new agreement on the Code of Conduct in the South China Sea (COC).

Third, the geographic proximity between China and Southeast Asian states, the size of their population, and the market scale of both sides set a good condition for China and ASEAN to jointly forge and enforce the value chains in a wide variety of areas to better serve the demands of the region and of the globe.[55]

More precisely, geographic proximity between China and Southeast Asia enables the cross-border movement of physical products relatively easier to reach each other's market. The more convenient and effective movement of goods not only promotes the development of the manufacturing industry, and in the meantime, it also drives the dynamics of other range of sectors such as the financial and insurance sector, and the shipping and delivery industry etc.[56]

Here is an example to prove the advantage of geographic proximity in helping facilitate trade connectivity - China's Guangdong province, based in the very southern part of China, and due to its proximity to Southeast Asia, has surpassed all other provinces of China in trading with ASEAN. The total trade volume between China's Guangdong province and ASEAN in 2020 amounted to $157.05 billion, constituting 22.9% of China's total trade with ASEAN, making ASEAN the largest trade partner of China's Guangdong province.[57]

Apart from that, the size of the skilled labour forces plus the market scale of both ASEAN and China including production and consumption capacity had enabled the two sides to enforce each other's capacity in supply and demands, and to enhance the interconnection of regional value chains in a variety of areas.

After all, the comparative advantages of China and Southeast Asian States in labour force, the size of population, geographic proximity, as well as the size of market are assumed to have played the most significant part in contributing to the flourish of economic and trade cooperation between the two sides since the beginning of the new century, which in the meantime has contributed to the success of regional integration. These factors will likely continue to play a crucial role in meeting the needs of ASEAN and China in the years ahead.

Apart from applying the above comparative advantages in helping forge connectivity and promote growth, there is also a need for the two sides to seek cooperation in more advanced science and technologies, in order to further pave the way for quality and deepened cooperation in a wider range of areas from a long-term perspective.

In addition to what China and ASEAN have achieved over the past decades, against the current historical context, China and ASEAN face new issues now, which, from an external dimension, mostly have a relevance to the forging and implementation of the strategies by major powers in the Indo-Pacific region, in particular, with regard to how the U.S. will likely conduct its strategy in the years ahead.

In line with the framework of the U.S. Indo-Pacific strategy, it will strive to seek new breakthroughs in a wide variety of areas such as issues related to supply chains, infrastructure, maritime security, and climate change etc.. Yet, given that the COVID-19 pandemic currently still generates a big impact on the world in various ways, it would be hardly for the U.S. to secure any concrete outcomes within a short-term in the aspects related to infrastructure and supply chains and so on. In this regard, in the near term, the U.S. would more likely take steps to focus on implementing the security aspect of its Indo-Pacific strategy. From the U.S. perspective, it should be the most effective means in helping enhance the U.S.- led alliance system and gather more strength.

The Taiwan issue over the past year has become a bit more contentious, as a result of a series of actions taken by the U.S.. It is one of the major factors in driving the rising tension between China and the U.S.. To move forward the implementation of the U.S. strategy, apart from playing the Taiwan card, as usual the U.S. would take further moves together with its allies under a series of security mechanisms such as the QUAD or the AUKUS.

In response to the new rounds of pressure, in addition to adhering to the core principles upheld by ASEAN and following the guidelines of the DOC, it is also in need for China and ASEAN to step up their negotiations on the COC.

It is generally assumed that the ASEAN Way in managing more

complicated situations, in particular in relation to extra-ASEAN affairs in the years to come, will continue to prove its effectiveness. By doing so, the ASEAN Way will be further consolidated, and so will be the ASEAN Centrality.

3.4 The United States and ASEAN

In the 19th century, as one of the late comers among the colonial powers, the U.S. had already started to be involved in the affairs related to Southeast Asia.

After having fought a number of devastating wars with the colonial powers as well as with the indigenous Southeast Asian people from time to time, the U.S. had turned itself from an aggressive colonizer, and then an imperial power, to a defender of justice during WWII by joining the efforts of Southeast Asian states in fighting against the Japanese aggression in Southeast Asia.

Throughout the Cold War period, the U.S. engagements with Southeast Asia, due to ideological confrontation with the Soviet Union-led socialist bloc, had mainly borne a purpose of curbing the influence of communism to this region. To meet that purpose, conflicts and wars between the two blocs respectively led by the U.S. and the Soviet Union had played a major role in dominating the evolution of Southeast Asian politics.

After the Cold War, the U.S. had, from a certain degree, shifted its focus away from Southeast Asia to other regions. Upon former U.S. President Bush's term, following the 9.11 terrorist attacks, the U.S. had adjusted the country's strategy by concentrating on the formulation and implementation of the U.S. "war on terror" policy. Then, issues related to the Middle East apparently had become a priority of the Bush Administration.

By the time when the Obama government assumed office, the whole western world was challenged by a serious global economic downturn. Meanwhile, the implementation of the series of policies in the Middle East including the U.S. invasion of Iraq met with an overwhelming criticism across the globe. Besides these, a new issue emerged and came to the U.S. attention - which was the rising role of China in Asia including China's increasing connectivity with its Southeast Asian neighbours. The new emerging situation, from the U.S. perspective, became a major challenge to the U.S. influence in

Southeast Asia, and further to the U.S. interest in maintaining its global hegemony. Against this background, the Obama Administration made a decision to turn away from the policy measures adopted by the Bush government to refocus on Asia.

In line with the U.S. refocusing on Asia strategy, concerning Southeast Asia more specifically, the U.S. government had moved quickly to re-engage with the countries in the region. During the first term of the Obama Administration, the U.S. had roughly taken the following significant actions toward the region: in February 2009, the U.S. then Secretary of State Hillary Clinton paid a visit to the Secretariat of ASEAN based in Jakarta, which was the first visit by a U.S. Secretary of State;[58] in July 2009, upon Mrs. Clinton's second trip to Southeast Asia for the ARF Foreign Ministerial, the U.S. and ASEAN signed the Treaty of Amity and Cooperation;[59] in 2010, the U.S. became a member of the East Asia Summit,[60] which is one of the significant forums led by ASEAN; in 2011, the U.S. set up a mission to ASEAN; in 2012, the U.S.-ASEAN meeting was upgraded to a leader's level.[61]

Then, through Obama's second term, the U.S. and ASEAN formed a strategic partnership in November 2015; further in 2016, the U.S. and ASEAN set up the U.S.-ASEAN Connect to better coordinate and meet the needs of the U.S. public - and private - sector economic initiatives in Southeast Asia.[62]

The series of crucial steps promptly taken by the Obama government were seen by some as "explicitly designed with 'symbolic diplomacy'", with a purpose of highlighting the U.S. special intention to re-engage Southeast Asia.[63]

After the Trump government assumed power, the U.S. government shifted away from a traditional style of the U.S. foreign policy. As guided by the "American First" policy, the Trump government, instead of highlighting the significance of the U.S.-led alliance system in serving the U.S. security interest, sought to prioritize the U.S. interest more in material or economic terms. To achieve that purpose, from occasion to occasion, the U.S. government had intended to act unilaterally by deploying various measures including launching trade wars. That foreign policy objective also meant that, through Trump's tenure, the U.S. government had relatively emphasized less of the security aspect of the U.S. foreign policy.

The Trump Administration released the U.S. Indo-Pacific strategy, the geographic scope and the issue areas covered by it were further broadened, compared to the strategy adopted by the previous government. By the time when Trump left office, the U.S. government was still at an early stage of striving to formulate the strategy and hadn't really started to implement it.

After the Biden Administration took office, the U.S. has started to take steps to conduct the Indo-Pacific strategy. Although it covers a wide variety of issues, the economic and security aspects of the strategy are obviously prioritized by the U.S. government. Ideally through implementing the Indo-Pacific strategy, from the U.S. perspective, the country would be able to exert a larger degree of domination in economic and security spheres in the Indo-Pacific region.

From the economic aspect, in May 2022, the U.S. together with a wide range of partners based in the Indo-Pacific region already launched an Indo-Pacific Economic Framework for Prosperity (IPEF) (Chapter 2 of this book contains more information about the IPEF). Besides that, toward Southeast Asia, so far the Biden Administration has subsequently announced a few batches of funds to aid the improvement of the relevant issue areas in the region, including a $102 million related to public health, economic initiatives, and climate change, a $150 million prioritizing on infrastructure and education etc., and a $60 million for maritime cooperation.[64]

From the security aspect, through implementing the Indo-Pacific strategy, the U.S. aims to forge a regional security architecture that would be able to serve the country's long-term strategic interest. Apparently, by solely participating in a range of ASEAN-led security mechanisms such as the ARF or the ADMM Plus, the U.S. goal of exerting a certain degree of control in the security field cannot be properly met. Therefore, the U.S. would rather intend to highlight the status of the U.S.-led security frameworks in order to achieve the U.S. security objective.

It is assumed that, to carry out the security aspect of the U.S. Indo-Pacific strategy, as usual, it would tend to deploy a series of frameworks such as the QUAD or the AUKUS or theU.S. treaty alliances. Apart from that, the Taiwan issue, as already briefly mentioned in the previous part, would be included in the U.S. security agenda as well. That means the U.S. would likely continue to use the Taiwan Card to help achieve the country's strategic interests. Further, the U.S. would try to get its allies and partners to be supportive of the U.S. security agenda.

The U.S. had ever attempted to shift the focus of the Asia Pacific

Economic Cooperation (APEC) from economic issues to security issues. However, that idea didn't meet the interests of regional states after all.[65] Besides that, the U.S. former Combatant Commander of the Asia-Pacific region Dennis Blair ever proposed a concept of "security communities" or "enhanced regional cooperation" to Southeast Asian states back in 2001. Nevertheless, countries in the region were not enthusiastic about this idea as well.[66]

To support the conduction of the U.S. Indo-Pacific strategy in the years ahead, the U.S. may tend to persuade ASEAN to back the U.S. various moves. However, very likely, for the interest of ASEAN as well as for the purpose of protecting regional peace and stability, ASEAN would strive to keep a position in accordance with the core principles upheld and practised by the organization. There might be differences between the U.S. and ASEAN from occasion to occasion in the coming years. ASEAN would most likely tend to apply the ASEAN Way rather than use any forceful means to settle the organization's differences with the U.S. to be possibly raised.

After all, the ASEAN Way doesn't mean to accommodate the strategies of great powers under all circumstances; rather, it means to protect the best interest of ASEAN. Some observers have depicted the ASEAN Way as a strategy or tactic of the organization.

In addition to the above, the territorial disputes in the South China Sea may continue to be an issue to be deployed by the U.S. in the process of carrying out its Indo-Pacific strategy. That means the U.S. may tend to leverage the situation by playing China's territorial disputes with its Southeast Asian neighbours.

Given that China and ASEAN have already reached a framework in handling the territorial disputes. By adhering to the framework, both sides have gained some experiences in managing the territorial disputes since the beginning of the new century. It is believed that the South China Sea disputes can be properly managed by China and the concerned Southeast Asian parties, alongside the process of the U.S. moving up the implementation of its Indo-Pacific strategy.

Based on the above analysis, therefore, the only issue that would risk sparking a serious consequence to the region would be related to Taiwan. The growing tension to be possibly generated by the Taiwan issue in the future would threat the ASEAN-led regional architecture. In the meantime, the rising tension derived from the Taiwan issue would also raise the difficulty for ASEAN, as a very important mediator in the region, in balancing the relationship among great powers.

To avoid the worst scenario taking place, in addition to let the ASEAN approach continue to play a role, there will be a need for China and the U.S. to work out a way to settle the Taiwan issue ultimately.

Forty-seven years ago, the end of the Vietnam War led to the departure of the U.S. from the soil of Vietnam. The U.S. departure didn't change the fact that, after all these years, the U.S. nowadays still keeps a close relevance to the region. Likewise, stopping meddling the relations between the Chinese mainland and Taiwan, and finding a proper way with China to promote the reunification of the country wouldn't alter the fact of the U.S. relevance to the region as well.

The most appropriate way to help sustain the U.S. relevance and influence in the Indo-Pacific would be to integrate the U.S. interest with that of other major powers in the region including China, rather than play against one another. For instance, given that China and the U.S. share a common concern in protecting the sea lanes in order to ensure maritime security, energy security, and freedom of navigation etc., the two countries can seek proper means to cooperate on these issues. Other concerned parties in the region can join the efforts made by the U.S. and China as well. After all, for the great interest of the Indo-Pacific region, as far as certain conditions are met, major powers should seek the possibility of deepening or expanding the areas of cooperation including both security and non-security issues.

In addition, the issue of whether the U.S. would be able to sustain its relevance in the Indo-Pacific region and beyond shouldn't necessarily mean the U.S. strong presence in the region in military and security terms; and crucially, it should also very much depend on the U.S. connectivity with the region from other wide variety of aspects such as social, economic, cultural, and people to people linkages etc. Prioritizing these aspects of the U.S. strategy while downplaying the traditional approach of the U.S. strategy would be conducive to the building of a new type of major power relations in the 21st century, as well as to the promotion and achievement of peaceful coexistence among all major powers.

Conclusion

This chapter has begun by exploring and analysing the historical and cultural origins of ASEAN and of the ASEAN Way. Obviously, what Southeast Asian states had experienced throughout a long historical period from the colonial era, and then the WWII, to the end of the Cold War had played a most significant part in leading to the founding of ASEAN and the shaping of the ASEAN Way.

Then, the research has mainly outlined some of the remarkable achievements made by ASEAN together with other major regional and international actors by adhering to the ASEAN approach. The new possible challenges faced by ASEAN in the process of managing both intra-ASEAN and extra-ASEAN affairs, against the new historical context, have been assessed in this part also. Further, the possible solutions and counter-arguments, in response to a variety of internal and external challenges, have been proposed as well.

Finally, this research has attempted to foresee the evolving trend of ASEAN's relations and engagements with the organization's key dialogue partners including India, Japan, China, and the United States.

Based on a deep observation and assessment from a wide range of dimensions, this chapter would make a concluding point that, against the current historical context, ASEAN's role and the ASEAN Way matter a lot in continuing to contribute to regional peace, stability, and economic progress in the Indo-Pacific region, and that the ASEAN Way has been proved to be a big strength of the organization in helping enhance the ASEAN Centrality, in mediating or balancing great power relations, as well as in helping forge an Indo-Pacific order and beyond.

Notes

1. For arguments regarding the function of ASEAN in addressing more contentious matters such as traditional security issue or human rights issue, please see Masahiro Kawai, Moe Thuzar, and Bill Hayton, "ASEAN's Regional Role and Relations with Japan: The Challenges of Deeper Integration", Research Paper, *Chatham House,* February 2016.

2. For analysis and arguments about ASEAN's role in driving regional integration at a more advanced level, please see European Foundation for South Asian Studies, "The ASEAN Way: Regional Integration Processes and

Limits to Integration in Southeast Asia", May 2021; also see Razak Nazir, "The ASEAN Way: What It Is, How It Must Change for the Future", *World Economic Forum*, 10 September 2018, https://europeansting.com/2018/09/10/the-asean-way-what-it-is-how-it-must-change-for-the-future/

3. Tekunan Susy, "The ASEAN Way: The Way to Regional Peace?", *Journal Hubungan International,* VOL. 3/ NO. 2, October 2014.

4. Rey Ty, "Colonialism and Nationalism in Southeast Asia", https://www.seasite.niu.edu/crossroads/ty/COLONIALISM_%20IN_SE%20ASIA.htm; also See Barton, Thomas F., Robert C. Kingsbury, and Gerald R. Showalter, *Southeast Asia Maps*, Chicago: Denoyer-Geppert Company, 1970; Fodor's, *Fodor's Southeast Asia,* New York: Fodor's Travel Guides, 1984.

5. Ibid.

6. Ibid.

7. Ibid.

8. Ibid.

9. Ibid; also see http://military-history.fandom.com/wiki/Dutch–Portuguese_War

10. European Foundation for South Asian Studies, "The ASEAN Way: Regional Integration Processes and Limits to Integration in Southeast Asia", May 2021.

11. Rey Ty, "Colonialism and Nationalism in Southeast Asia", https://www.seasite.niu.edu/crossroads/ty/COLONIALISM_%20IN_SE%20ASIA.htm

12. Ibid.

13. European Foundation for South Asian Studies, "The ASEAN Way: Regional Integration Processes and Limits to Integration in Southeast Asia", May 2021.

14. Ibid.

15. Adli Hazmi, "What Is 'ASEAN Way'", 21 January 2020, https://seasia.co/2020/01/21/what-is-asean-way

16. *European Foundation for South Asian Studies,* "The ASEAN Way: Regional Integration Processes and Limits to Integration in Southeast Asia", May 2021.

17. Ibid.

18. Ibid.

19. Association of Southeast Asian Nations, "The ASEAN Declaration (Bangkok Declaration)", Bangkok, Thailand, 8 August 1967, https://agreement.asean.org/media/download/20140117154159.pdf

20. Ibid.

21. Ibid.

22. Steve Jones, "The Geneva Accords of 1954 - There Was Little Agreement over This Agreement", *ThoughtCo,* updated on 31 March 2019, https://www.thoughtco.com/the-geneva-accords-1954-3310118

23. Ibid.

24. Ibid.

25. Adli Hazmi, "What Is "ASEAN Way", 21 January 2020, https://seasia.co/2020/01/21/what-is-asean-way

26. Ibid.

27. Ibid.

28. Ibid.

29. Ibid.

30. Vaughn Bruce and Morrison M. Wayne, "China-Southeast Asia Relations: Trends, Issues, and implications for the United States", RL32688, P6, *Congressional Research Service*, 2006.

31. Razak Nazir, "The ASEAN Way: What It Is, How It Must Change for the Future", *World Economic Forum*, 10 September 2018, https://europeansting.com/2018/09/10/the-asean-way-what-it-is-how-it-must-change-for-the-future/

32. Ibid.

33. Ibid.

34. Karishma, "India-ASEAN Relations: Evolution, Challenges & Recent Developments", *IAS Express,* 30 December 2019, https://www.iasexpress.net/india-asean-relations/

35. Fung Doris, "The Growing China-ASEAN Economic Ties", *HKTDC Research,* 07 Jan 2022, https://research.hktdc.com/en/article/OTUxMzk0NDE0

36. "India-ASEAN Relations", *IAS Academy,* 18 March 2022, https://civils360.com/2022/03/18/india-asean-relations/

37. Karishma, "India-ASEAN Relations: Evolution, Challenges & Recent Developments", *IAS Express,* 30 December 2019, https://www.iasexpress.net/india-asean-relations/

38. Ibid.

39. "India-ASEAN Relations", *IAS Academy,* 18 March 2022, https://civils360.com/2022/03/18/india-asean-relations/

40. "ASEAN-India: Economic Connectivity", 31 January 2019, https://indiafoundation.in/articles-and-commentaries/asean-india-economic-

connectivity/

41. Association of Southeast Asian Nations, "ASEAN-India Economic Relations -Overview", https://asean.org/our-communities/economic-community/ integration-with-global-economy/asean-india-economic-relations/

42. "India-ASEAN Relations", *IAS Academy,* 18 March 2022, https://civils 360.com/2022/03/18/india-asean-relations/

43. Ibid.

44. Ibid.

45. Karishma, "India-ASEAN Relations: Evolution, Challenges & Recent Develo pments", *IAS Express,* 30 December 2019, https://www. Iasexpre ss.net/india-asean-relations/

46. "ASEAN-India: Economic Connectivity", 31 January 2019, https:// indiafoundation.in/articles-and-commentaries/asean-india-economic-connectivity/

47. Association of Southeast Asian Nations, "ASEAN-Japan Economic Relations -Overview", https://asean.org/our-communities/economic-community/ integration-with-global-economy/asean-jap an-economic-relation/

48. Masashi Nishihara, "Japan's Political and Security Relations with ASEAN", ASEAN-Japan Cooperation: A Foundation for East Asian Community; (ed. Japan Centre for International Exchanges), Tokyo: Japan Centre for International Exchange, 2003, P155.

49. Mie Oba, "Japan-ASEAN Cooperation: A Central Element of East Asia's Regional Architecture", 1 September, http://www.nip pon.com /en/c urrents/d00345

50. Masashi Nishihara, "Japan's Political and Security Relations with ASEAN", ASEAN-Japan Cooperation : A Foundation for East Asian Community; (ed. Japan Centre for International Exchanges), Tokyo: Japan Centre for International Exchange, 2003.

51. Ibid, P157.

52. Masahiro Kawai, Moe Thuzar, and Bill Hayton, "ASEAN's Regional Role and Relations with Japan: The Challenges of Deeper Integration", Research Paper, P28, *Chatham House,* February 2016.

53. "China Remains ASEAN's Largest Trading Partner", *China Daily,* 30 August 2022, http://www.chinadaily.com.cn/a/202208/30/WS630d74bda310fd2 b29e74f93.html

54. Fung Doris, "The Growing China-ASEAN Economic Ties", *HKTDC Research,* 07 Jan 2022, https://research.hktdc.com/en/article/OTUxMzk0NDE0

55. Regarding the detailed examples of how China and Southeast Asian

countries jointly forge the regional value chains in a variety of areas, please see Richard Pomfret, "Economic Relations between China and ASEAN", 13 September 2017 http://www.theasiadialogue.com /2017/09 /13/economic-relations-between-china-and-asean/

56. Ibid.

57. Fung Doris, "The Growing China-ASEAN Economic Ties", *HKTDC Research,* 07 Jan 2022, https://research.hktdc.com/en/article/OTUxMzk0NDE0

58. Lum Thomas and Dolven Ben et al., "United States Relations with the Association of Southeast Asian Nations (ASEAN)", *Congressional Research Service,* R40933, P2, 12 March 2010.

59. Ibid, P2.

60. Dolven Ben, "The Association of Southeast Asian Nations (ASEAN)", *Congressional Research Service*, IF10348, 26 July 2022.

61. Ibid.

62. Ibid.

63. Lum Thomas and Dolven Ben et al., "United States Relations with the Association of Southeast Asian Nations (ASEAN)", *Congressional Research Service,* R40933, P2, 12 March 2010.

64. Dolven Ben, "The Association of Southeast Asian Nations (ASEAN)", *Congressional Research Service*, IF10348, 26 July 2022.

65. Vaughn Bruce and Morrison M. Wayne, "China-Southeast Asia Relations: Trends, Issues, and implications for the United States", *Congressional Research Service*, RL32688, P26, 2006.

66. Ibid, P26.

Conclusion

This project has explored and assessed the crucial factors and issues that could affect the likely trend of the relations among major powers and entities as well as the power structure in the years ahead at both regional and international levels. Four topics consisting of the North Korean nuclear issue and its impact on the possible shaping of a Northeast Asia regional security order, the trilateral relations of Japan, China, and the U.S. and their relevance to the forging of an Indo-Pacific order, the Ukraine crisis and the prospect of forging a new European order, as well as ASEAN's role in the process of shaping an Indo-Pacific order were selected to serve the research purpose of this project.

Regarding the connection between the North Korean nuclear issue and the Northeast Asian security order, this study concluded that three core factors, consisting of leadership transitions especially in the U.S., North Korea, and South Korea , external environment, and the growing sensitivity of the North Korean nuclear issue itself, have so far been proved to play a crucial role in having significantly caused a delay of the Korean Peninsula peace process; and that the root cause of the North Korean nuclear issue lies in the fact that North Korea is afraid of being invaded by the U.S., while the U.S. is worried about losing its influence on the Korean Peninsular. Therefore, to meet the U.S. interest, the U.S. real intention over the North Korean nuclear issue is to denuclearize North Korea while guarantee the U.S. relevance on the Korean Peninsula.

To move forward the Korean Peninsula peace process and to meet the interests of all the parties concerned, this study has proposed two solutions, one of which would be related to promoting institutional building, through which, the major stakeholders jointly set up a special mechanism/institution to focus on dealing with the Korean Peninsula nuclear issue. It can be an Ad Hoc one, and can also adopt some experiences accumulated by the Six Party Talks, yet obviously it would be empowered by the main stakeholders to charge all the matters related to the Korean Peninsula peace process. In this case, the special institution would be set in a primary position to direct the development of the North Korean nuclear issue. Another solution would be involved in the function of great power coordination/consultation mechanism - more precisely, great powers jointly provide North Korea with security guarantee as well as help North Korea's economy alongside the denuclearization process, in exchange, for denuclearization of the Korean Peninsula step by step.

Every solution needs to take a number of steps and also needs to devote a great deal of diplomatic efforts. More than three decades have passed, there are still full of uncertainties toward the final settlement of the North Korean nuclear issue. It is assumed that the approach the current one or a more inclusive and creative one - taken by the U.S. would matter more significantly in determining how the issue can be properly addressed in the end.

With regard to the second selected topic, the trilateral engagements of the U.S., China, and Japan as well as their impacts on the possible shaping of an Indo-Pacific order, this research has tended to observe whether there could be an alternative beyond the traditional narratives of U.S.-Japan relations in all respects. Then, it reached a point that even though Japan would still depend on the protection of the U.S. in traditional security terms, yet Japan has managed to pursue more alternative means to better serve Japan's interest. For instance, Japan has worked out its own Indo-Pacific vision, and in the meantime tended to persuade more partners to support Japan's agenda. Apart from working with the U.S. on security issues, Japan has also sought to work more closely with other partners such as India and Australia etc. on security issues in order to create more certainties for Japan.

In addition to the efforts made related to security, Japan has sought to use its economic and technological power to help further expand Japan's reach to other regions such as Africa and the Middle East.

Along with the whole process of implementing Japan's Indo-Pacific agenda, the China factor cannot be ignored, given that Japan and China would as usual keep a close economic relationship in the years ahead. Therefore, from Japan's perspective, to meet Japan's strategic interest, this country would tend to make a balance between its economic interest and security interest and between its relations with the U.S. and with other various partners.

Whether Japan would be able to successfully manage such a balance in the process of carrying out its Indo-Pacific vision would not only greatly affect Japan's status in regional and international affairs, but also would likely have an impact on the power structure at both regional and global levels.

In relation to the Ukraine crisis and its impact on the prospect of forging a new European order, this project has reached a point that the settlement of the Ukraine crisis, apart from greatly affecting Russia-Ukraine relations, would also likely have a big impact on the U.S.-EU, U.S.-Russia, as well as Russia-EU relations. This study has also analysed in great details of the root cause of the Ukraine crisis, which lied in the continuity of the U.S. Cold War policy toward Russia.

In the meantime, from the Ukrainian side, the real issue faced by the country is not about what system Ukraine has adopted, rather, it is about how to make the system function more effectively to serve the country's best interest. Generally, over the past years, there has been a low level of trust within the Ukrainian society toward the government capacity in delivering relevant reforms. Therefore, the Marshall Plan carried out by the U.S. toward Western Europe after WWII hasn't so far suited Ukraine's case well.

Due to the growing complication of the Ukraine crisis, possible bilateral settlement of the crisis by Russia and Ukraine appears to be getting more difficult. The issue of whether major European powers are able to take a lead in affecting the trend of the Ukraine crisis would not only cause a big impact on the strategic autonomy of Europe, but also matter significantly to the possible forging of a new European order. So, handling the Ukraine crisis can be a big test for the collective capacity of major European powers.

At the moment, the U.S. position on and involvement in the Ukraine crisis still matter a very significant part in affecting the development trend of the Ukraine issue. Therefore, in a long-term, there is no clear picture about how the crisis can be finally settled. Only if the U.S. and its western allies and partners would decide to adjust their current positions and policies toward Ukraine, reaching a ceasefire agreement at an earlier date might be possible.

Concerning the linkage between the ASEAN Way and the prospect of forging an Indo-Pacific order, this study has made a point that, given that ASEAN has made tremendous achievements including in the aspect of contributing to regional peace, stability, and economic progress by applying the ASWEAN Way since the founding of the organization, ASEAN would strive to sustain the ASEAN Way in managing both intra-ASEAN and extra-ASEAN affairs, even though the organization would likely face a growing challenge in doing so in the years ahead.

In addition to that, against the new regional and global context, ASEAN's role would likely be further highlighted; and major powers having a relevance to the Indo-Pacific region such as India, Japan, China, and the U.S. would attach greater importance to ASEAN's position in the process of carrying out their agendas respectively, largely because they would take ASEAN as a very significant stabilizing force in contributing to regional peace and stability by playing a balancing role among major powers.

In a speech made by Russian President Putin upon the 19th Annual Meeting of the Valdai International Discussion Club, he indicated that "we are standing at a historical milestone, ahead of what is probably the most dangerous, unpredictable and at the same time important decade since the end of WWII."[1] In facing the upcoming turbulence, Mr. Putin also said that we either "continue to accumulate a burden of problems that will inevitably crush us all, or to try together to find solutions, albeit imperfect, but working, capable of making our world safer and more stable."[2]

Jointly forging a "truly democratic multi-polar world"[3], in line with which, to promote the rule of law, justice, fairness, and freedom, mutual cooperation, and inclusive and quality development at the international stage, could be a sound alternative solution to address the challenges encountered by humankind after all.

Notes

1. "'No One Can Sit Out the Coming Storm': Putin's Milestone Valdai Speech", *RT,* 27 October 2022, https://www.rt.com/russia/565476-putin-valdai-club-takeaways/, for the full speech of Russian President Putin at the 19th annual meeting of the Valdai International Discussion Club, please see en.kremlin.ru/events/president/news/69695
2. Ibid.
3. Ibid.

Bibliography

Albert Eleanor (2019). "North Korean Nuclear Negotiations", *Council on Foreign Relation,* 2 July 2019, https://www.cfr.org/timeline/north-korean-nuclear-negotiations

Archick Kristin and Mix E. Derek (2015). "U.S.-EU Cooperation on Ukraine and Russia", *Congressional Research Service,* IN10129, 13 March 2015.

Association of Southeast Asian Nations (1967). "The ASEAN Declaration (Bangkok Declaration)", Bangkok, Thailand, 8 August 1967, https://agreeme nt.asean.org/media/download/20140117154159.pdf

Association of Southeast Asian Nations, "ASEAN-Japan Economic Relations - Overview", https://asean.org/our-communities/economic-community/integration-wi th-global-economy/asea n-japan-economic-relation/

Association of Southeast Asian Nations, "ASEAN-India Economic Relations - Overview", https://asean.org/our-communities/economic-community/integration-wi th-global-economy/asea n-india-economic-relations/

Barton,Thomas F., Robert C. Kingsbury, and Gerald R. Showalter (1970). *Southeast Asia Maps*, Chicago: Denoyer-Geppert Company.

Ben Dolven (2022). "The Association of Southeast Asian Nations (ASEAN)", *Congressional Research Service*, IF10348, 26 July 2022.

Bink Addy (2022). "How Much Oil Will Be Left in the US Strategic Reserve after Biden's Release?", *NewsNation,* 31 March 2022, https://www.newsnationnow.com/us-news/how-much-oil-will-be-left-in-the-us-strategic-reserve- after-bidens-release/

Boghani Priyanka (2019). "The U.S. and North Korea on the Brink: A Timeline", 28 February 2019, http://www.pbs.org/wgbh/frontline/article/the-u-s-and-north-korea-on-the-brink-a-timeline/

Bruce Vaughn and Wayne M. Morrison (2006). "China-Southeast Asia Relations: Trends, Issues, and implications for the United States", *Congressional Research Service*, RL32688, 2006.

CBS News (2022). "OPEC Maintains Oil Targets amid Uncertainty over Russian Sanctions", 4 December 2022, https://www.cbsnews.com/news/opec-oil-production-russia-sanctions/

Chiang Min-Hua (2019). "Contemporary China-Japan Relations: the Politically Driven Economic Linkage", *East Asia (2019),* 36:285, Springer.

China Daily (2022). "China Remains ASEAN's Largest Trading Partner", *China Daily,* 30 August 2022, http://www.chinadaily.com.cn/a/202208/30/WS630d74bda310fd2b29e74f93.html

Cooper H. William (2014). "U.S.-Japan Economic Relations: Significance, Prospects, and Policy Options", *Congressional Research Service*, 18 February 2014.

Council of the European Union (2022). "Timeline-EU Response to Russia's Invasion of Ukraine", https://www.Consilium.europa.eu/en/policies/eu-response-ukraine-invasion/timeline-eu-respons e-ukraine-invasion

Council of the European Union (2022). "Infographic - How Much Gas Have the EU Countries Stored?", https://www.consilium.europa.eu/en/infographics/gas-storage-capacity/

Council on Foreign Relations, "A Conversation with Jake Sullivan", http://www.cfr.org/event/conversation-jake-sullivan;

Credinform (2018). "Russia Continues to Diversify the Economy", 4 May 2018, http://credinform.ru/en-GB/Publications/Herald/8fd8420dda03

Dabrowski Marek et al. (2020). "Ukraine: Trade Reorientation from Russia to the EU", 13 July 2020, http://www.bruegel.org/2020/07/ukraine-trade-reorientation-from-russia-to-the-eu/

Dong Yan and Xu Qiyuan (2020). "Staying the Course of Deepening Reform and Opening-up in Facing the U.S.-China Trade War", Shanghai Pushan Foundation, February 2020.

Doris Fung (2022). "The Growing China-ASEAN Economic Ties", *HKTDC Research,* 07 Jan 2022, https://research.hktdc.com/en/article/OTUxMzk0NDE0

Dragneva Rilka and Wolczuk Kataryna (2012). "Russia, the Eurasian Customs Union and the EU: Cooperation, Stagnation or Rivalry?", Briefing Paper, *Chatham House*, August 2012.

European Commission, "EU Trade Relations with Russia", http://policy.trade.ec.europa.eu/eu-trade-relationships-country-and-region/countries-and-region s/russia_en

European Foundation for South Asian Studies (2021). "The ASEAN Way: Regional Integration Processes and Limits to Integration in Southeast Asia", May 2021.

Fischer Sabine (2007). "The EU and Russia: Conflict and Potentials of a Difficult Partnership", *SWP Research Paper,* German Institute for International and Security Affairs, January 2007.

Fodor's (1984). *Fodor's Southeast Asia,* New York: Fodor's Travel Guides.

Hazmi Adli (2020). "What Is 'ASEAN Way'", 21 January 2020, https://seasia.co/2020/01/21/what-is-asean-way

Hoff Rachel, "Next Steps for U.S.-Japan Security Cooperation", *SASAKAWA USA.*

IAS Academy (2022). "India-ASEAN Relations", 18 March 2022, https://civils360.com/2022/03/18/india-asean-relations/

India Foundation (2019). "ASEAN-India: Economic Connectivity", 31 January 2019, https://indiafoundation.in/articles-and-commentaries/asean-india-economic-connectivity/

Interfax (2022). "IMF Forecasts Decline in Ukraine's GDP by 35%", 19 April 2022, http://interfax.com/newsroom/top-stories/78378/

Ji Da-gyum (2021). "U.S. Seeks 'step-by-step' Approach toward Denuclearization", *The Korea Herald,* 19 December 2021, http://www.koreaherald.com/view.php?ud=20211219000150

Jones Steve (2019). "The Geneva Accords of 1954 - There Was Little Agreement over This Agreement", *ThoughtCo,* updated on 31 March 2019, https://www.thoughtco.com/the-geneva-accords-1954-3310118

Karishma (2019). "India-ASEAN Relations: Evolution, Challenges & Recent Developments", *IAS Express,*
30 December 2019, https://www.iasexpress.net/india-asean-relations/

Kawai Masahiro, Thuzar Moe, and Hayton Bill (2016). "ASEAN's Regional Role and Relations with Japan: The Challenges of Deeper Integration", Research Paper, *Chatham House,* February 2016.

Kissinger Henry (2022). "Henry Kissinger's speech at the World Economic Forum in Davos", *Ukrainian Institute of Strategies of Global Development and Adaptation*, 26 May 2022, https://uisgda.com/en/rech-genri-kissindzhera-na-vsemirnom-ekonomicheskom-forume-v-davose. html

Kuo Yujen, "Japan's Roles in the Indo-Pacific Strategy", *Prospect Journal,* NO. 19: 29, https://www.pf.org.tw/files/6236/8B3BC62D-6F19-4E23-8D96-3BBC3 04 2464F

Mazneva Elena and Shiryaevskaya Anna (2022). "EU Is Hooked on Russia LNG", *Bloomberg,*
https://www.rigzone.com/news/wire/eu_is_hooked_on_russia_lng-30-nov-2022-171221-article/

Mission of Japan to ASEAN, "A New Foreign Policy Strategy: 'A free and open Indo-Pacific Strategy'",
https://www.asean.emb-japan.go.jp/files/000352880.pdf

Morelli L. Vincent (2017). "Ukraine: Current Issues and U.S. Policy", *Congressional Research Service*, RL33460, 3 January 2017.

Nezam Joshua (2021). "An End-of-War Declaration on the Korean Peninsula: Pursuing a Phased Agreement with the Goal of Complete Denucle arization", *Interview with Shin-wha Lee,* The National Bureau of Asian Research, 3 December 2021,
https://www.nbr.org/publication/an-end-of-war-declaration-on-the-korean-peninsula-pursuing-a-phased-agreement-with-the-goal-of-comp lete-denuclearization/

Nishihara Masashi (2003). "Japan's Political and Security Relations with ASEAN", ASEAN-Japan Cooperation: A Foundation for East Asian Community; (ed. Japan Centre for International Exchanges), Tokyo: Japan Centre for International Exchange.

Oba Mie, "Japan-ASEAN Cooperation: A Central Element of East Asia's Regional Architecture", 1 September, http://www.nippon.com/en/currents/ d00 34 5

Office of the United States Trade Representative (2022). "The Indo-Pacific Economic Framework for Prosperity: Biden-Harris Administration's Negotiating Goals for the Connected Economy (Trade) Pillar", 23 September 2022,
https://ustr.gov/aboutus/policyoffices/pressoffice/pressreleases/2022/se ptember/indo-pacific-economic-framework-prosperity-biden-harris-administrations-negotiating-goals-connected

O'keefe Ed and Melissa Quinn (2022). "Biden Administration Asks Congress for $32.5 billion for COVID and Ukraine", *CBS News,* 4 March 2022,
http://www.cbsnews.com/news/ukraine-aid-biden-administration-congress-covid/

Padilla Ramon (2022). "As Global Oil Production Is Reduced, Will Gas Prices Increase or Decrease? The Answer Is Mixed", *USA TODAY*, 20 October 2022,
https://www.usatoday.com/in-depth/graphics/2022/10/19/oil-production-reduction-gas-prices-g raphics/10478122002/

Padilla Ramon (2022). "Where Are the US Strategic Oil Reserves? Here's How Many Barrels Remain and Where They Are", *USA TODAY,* 21 October 2022,
https://www.usatoday.com/in-depth/graphics/2022/10/19/how-long-us-oil-reserves-last-size-sup ply-amid-record-low/10541808002/

Pomfret Richard (2017). "Economic Relations between China and ASEAN", 13 September 2017, http://www.theasiadialogue.com/2017/09/13/economic relations-between-china-and-asean/

Razak Nazir (2018). "The ASEAN Way: What It Is, How It Must Change for the Future", *World Economic Forum*, 10 September 2018. https://europeansting.com/2018/09/10/the-asean-way-what-it-is-how-it-must-change-for-the-fu ture/

Robertson Lori (2022). "U.S. Aid to Ukraine, Explained", 2 December 2022, https://www.factcheck.org/2022/12/u-s-aid-to-ukraine-explained/

Rumer Eugene and Sokolsky Richard (2019). "Thirty Years of U.S. Policy toward Russia: Can the Vicious Circle Be Broken?", *Carnegie Endowment,* 20 June 2019.

Russia Today (2022). "Russia Issues New Estimate of Ukrainian Combat Losses", https://www.rt.com/russia/567764-russia-ukraine-combat-losses/

Russia Today (2022). "Merkel Doubles down on Ukraine Peace Revelations", 28 December 2022, https://www.rt.com/news/569036-merkel-minsk-accords-ukraine/

Russia Today (2022). "US Reveals Value of Frozen Russian Assets", https://www.rt.com/business/558076-frozen-russian-assets-amount-revealed/

Russia Today (2022). "Time for Ukraine talks 'not right now' - White House", https://www.rt.com/news/568398-sullivan-ukraine-talks-russia/

Russia Today (2022). "US Reveals Value of Frozen Russian Assets", https://www.rt.com/business/558076-frozen-russian-assets-amount-revealed/

Russia Today (2022). "'No One Can Sit Out the Coming Storm': Putin's Milestone Valdai Speech", 27 October 2022, https://www.rt.com /russia/565476-putin-valdai-club-takeaways/

Russell Martin (2022). "U.S.-Russia Relations - Geopolitical, Security, Economic, and Human Dimensions", *European Parliamentary Research Service,* https://www.europarl.europa.eu/RegData/etudes/BRIE/2022/698919/EP RS_BRI(2022)698919_E N.pdf

Scoh W. Harold (2020). "Regional Responses to U.S.-China Competition in the Indo-Pacific", *RAND.*

Seo Yoonjung, Jeong Sophie, Ogura Junko, and Whiteman Hilary (2022). "North Korea Fired the Highest Number of Short-range Missiles in A Day, Says South Korea", *CNN*, 2 November 2022, https://edition.cnn.com/2022/11 /01 /asia/north-korea-missiles-wednesday-intl-hnk/index.html

Semler Bystephen (2022). "The Ukraine Aid Bill Is A Massive Windfall for U.S. Military Contractors", 26 May 2022, http://www.jacobinmag.com/2022/05/ukraine-aid-bill-congress-biden-military-health

Sputniknews (2022). "Europe's Imports of Russian LNG Increase by 42% in 2022, Report Suggests",
https://sputniknews.com/20221129/europes-imports-of-russian-lng-increase-by-42-in-2022-repo rt-suggests-1104807087.html

Statista (2022). "Russia: Inflation rate from September 2021 to October 2022 (compared to the same month of the previous year)",
https://www.statista.com/statistics/276323/monthly-inflation-rate-in-russia/

Statista (2022). "Closing Price of Brent, OPEC Basket, and WTI Crude Oil at the Beginning of Each Week from 2 March 2020 to 28 December 2022 (in U.S. dollars per barrel)", https://www.statista.com/statistics/326017/weekly-crude-oil-prices/

Statista (2022). "Number of Border Crossings between Ukraine and the Countries Selected, alongside the Russia-Ukraine War between 24 February and 29 November 2022 (in 1,000s)", https://www.statista.com/statistics/12934 03/cee-ukrainian-refugees-by-country/

Statista (2022). "Monthly Natural Gas Price Index Worldwide from January 2020 to October 2022", https://www.statista.com/statistics/1302994/monthly-natural-gas-price-index-worldwide/

Statista (2022). "Liquefied Natural Gas (LNG) Exports from the United States from 2018 to 2022, with A Forecast Until 2023", https://www.statista.com/statistics/1099336/us-liquefied-natural-gas-exports/

Stockholm Institute of Transition Economics (2022). "What Are the Effects of Banning Russian Oil and Gas across the EU?", 29 April 2022,
https://www.hhs.se/en/about-us/news/site-publications/2022/what-are-the-effects-of-banning-r ussian-oil-and-gas-across-the-eu/

Tekunan Susy (2014). "The ASEAN Way: The Way to Regional Peace?", *Journal Hubungan International,* VOL. 3/NO.2, October 2014.

The Diplomatic Service of the European Union (2021). "Facts and Figures about EU-Russia Relations",
http://www.eeas.europa.eu/sites/default/files/eeas-eu-russia_relation-en_2021-07.pdf

The White House (2009). "President Barack Obama's Inaugural Address", 21 January 2009, https://obamawhitehouse.archives.gov/blog/2009/01/21/presiden t-barack-obamas-inaugural-address

The White House (2022). "Fact Sheet on U.S. Security Assistance for Ukraine", 16 March 2022, http://www.whitehouse.gov/briefing-room/sta tements-releases/2022/03/16/fact-sheet-on-u-s-s ecurity-assistance-for-ukraine/

The White House (2022). "Indo-Pacific Strategy of the United States", 11 February 2022, https://www.whitehouse.gov/wp-content/uploads/2022 /02/ U.S. -Indo-Pacific-Strategy.pdf

The White House (2022). "FACT SHEET: In Asia, President Biden and A Dozen Indo-Pacific Partners Launch the Indo-Pacific Economic Framework for Prosperity", 23 May 2022, https://www.whitehouse.gov/briefing-room/s tatements-releases/2022/05/23/fact-sheet-in-asia-president-biden-and-a-dozen-indo-pacific-partners-launch-the-indo-pacific-economic-framew ork- for-prosperity/

Thomas Lum and Ben Dolven et al. (2010). "United States Relations with the Association of Southeast Asian Nations (ASEAN)", *Congressional Research Service,* R40933, 12 March 2010.

TxT (2022). "The War Cost the Ukrainian Economy \$600 billion", 19 April 2022, https://www.txtreport.com/news/2022-04-19-the-war-cost-the-ukrainian -economy-%24-600-billi on.rJANBosVq.html=

Ty Rey, "Colonialism and Nationalism in Southeast Asia", https:// www.seasite.niu.edu/crossroads/ty/COLONIALISM_%20IN_SE%20ASIA.ht m

United Nations High Commissioner for Refugees (2022). "Where We Are Now: 100 Days of Crisis in Ukraine", http://www.unrefugees.org/news/where-we-are-now-100-days-of-crisis-in-ukraine/

U.S. Department of Energy (2022). "U.S. and 30 Countries Commit to Release 60 Million Barrels of Oil From Strategic Reserves to Stabilize Global Energy Markets", 1 March 2022, https://www.energy.gov/articles/us-and-30-countries-commit-release-60-million-barrels-oil-strategic-reserves-stabili ze

Vidyashree S (2022). "Ukraine Economy to Shrink by 45.1% in 2022, Russia's GDP to Drop by 11.2%: World Bank", *Republicworld,* 11 April 2022, http://www.republicworld.com/world-news/russia-ukraine-crisis/ukraine-economy-to-shrink-by-45-dot-1-percent-in-2022-russias-gdp-to-drop-by-11-dot-2-percent-world-bank-articleshow.html

Wertz Daniel (2017). "Inter-Korean Relations", *ISSUE BRIEF,* The National Committee of North Korea.

Wit Joel (2001). "The United States and North Korea", *The Brookings,* 15 March 2001,
http://www.brookings.edu/research/the-united-states-and-north-korea/

Yoshida Fumihiko and Paik Haksoon (2020). "From Peace on the Korean Peninsula to a Northeast Asia Nuclear Weapon Free Zone", *Journal for Peace and Nuclear Disarmament*, VOL. 3/NO.1: 123-128, 2020,
https://www.tandfonline.com/doi/epdf/10.1080/25751654.2020.1747910?needAccess=true&rol e=button

Author

Jin Ran is Founder and Director of the Centre for Strategic Thinking, which is an independent and non-profit driven research and advisory think tank, focusing on research and analysis on a range of topics related to global governance, great power relations, foreign policy, as well as economic and trade issues etc. Prior to that, Jin had worked at a few governmental and inter-governmental organizations including with the Asian Development Bank's Regional Knowledge Sharing Initiative as a Knowledge Sharing Officer, and then with the Embassy of Canada to China as a Foreign Policy Specialist.

9 783757 513078